THIS OTHER EDEN

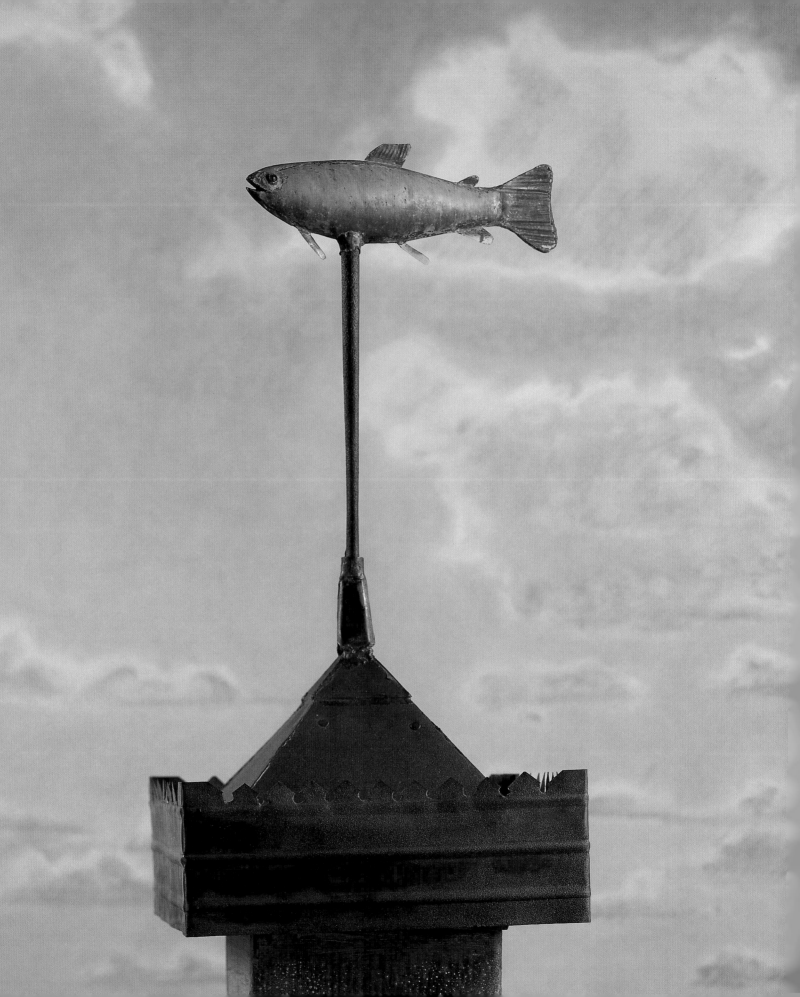

PHIL TILNEY

Foreword by Bill Richardson

This Other Eden

CANADIAN FOLK ART OUTDOORS

DOUGLAS & MCINTYRE
VANCOUVER/TORONTO

CANADIAN MUSEUM OF CIVILIZATION
HULL, QUEBEC

The Douglas & McIntyre Publishing Group
2323 Quebec Street, Suite 201
Vancouver, British Columbia v5T 4s7

Canadian Cataloguing in Publication Data
Tilney, Philip V. R.
  This other eden

  Copublished by: Canadian Museum of Civilization.
  Includes bibliographical references.
  ISBN 1–55054–732–1 (bound). ISBN 1–55054–698–8 (pbk.)

   1. Folk Art—Canada. 2. Garden ornaments and furniture—Canada.
 I. Canadian Museum of Civilization. II. Title.
NK841.T54 1999   745.5'0971   C99–910262–1

Editing by Catherine Bennett
Cover and text design by Peter Cocking
Front and back cover photographs by Harry Foster
Publication coordination at Canadian Museum of Civilization by Anne Malépart
Printed and bound in Canada by Friesens
Printed on acid-free paper ∞

This book is published in conjunction with *This Other Eden: Canadian Folk Art Outdoors,* a national touring exhibition, organized by the Canadian Museum of Civilization and made possible by Investors Group. The project sponsorship has been coordinated by Arts & Communications under the direction of Janet Conover.

The publisher gratefully acknowledges the assistance of the Canada Council for the Arts and of the British Columbia Ministry of Tourism, Small Business and Culture. The publisher also acknowledges the financial support of the Government of Canada through the Book Publishing Industry Development Program for its publishing activities.

p. ii: Monsieur A. Durangeau of La Prairie, Quebec, made this brook trout weather vane ventilator to decorate his fishing camp. After mounting it on his home to see how it looked, he never got around to removing it. (Harry Foster; CMC 77-945)

To Magnús Einarsson: Folklorist and Friend, 1941–1998

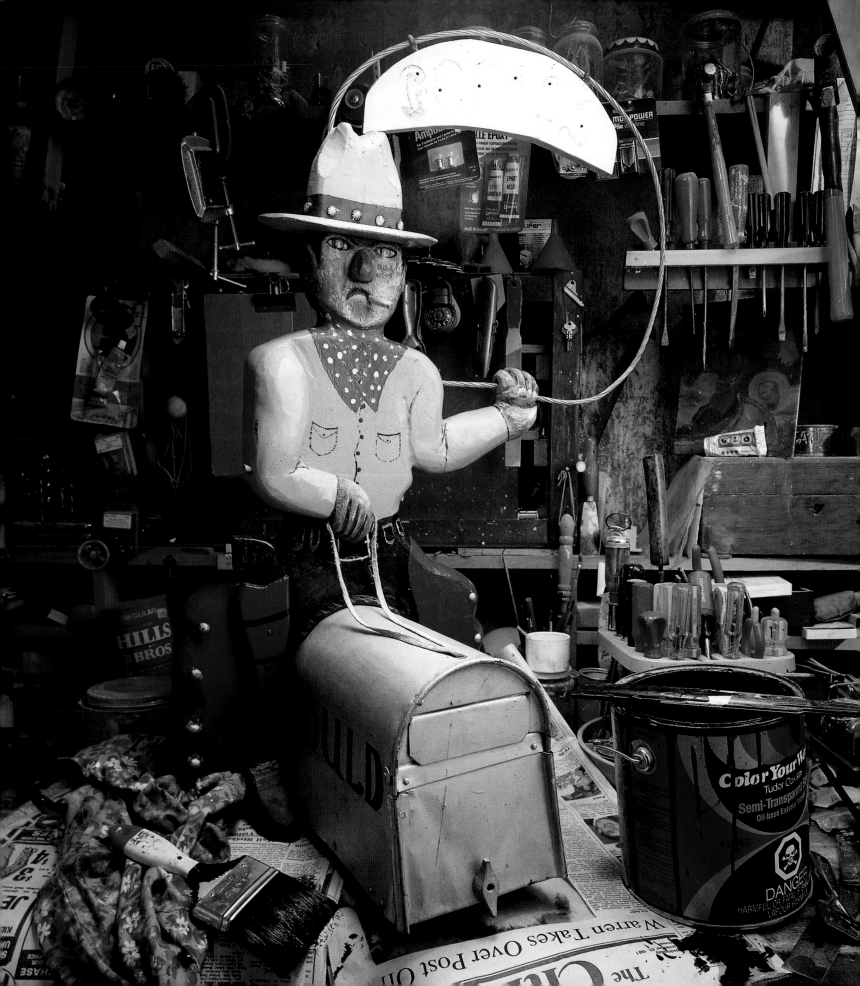

The decorated mailbox is a powerful and widespread genre of outdoor folk art. Mr. Gould's delightful, bandy-legged cowboy adorned his mailbox in Duntroon, Ontario, for many years. Decoration has added aesthetic value to the object's utilitarian function. (Harry Foster)

Table of Contents

Seventy Years of History 2

A Vast Landscape Writ Small 6

Foreword 9

Acknowledgements 15

Chapter One   **Folk Art in the Garden: Today and Yesterday** 17

Chapter Two   **Folklore and Folk Art: Indoors and Out** 33

Chapter Three   **Canadian Folk Art Outdoors** 61

Chapter Four   **From the Garden of Eden to Eden in the Garden** 85

Chapter Five   **The Morphing of Folk Art and the Canadian Garden** 117

Bibliography 130

Seventy Years of History

IF YOU HAVE EVER taken a leisurely drive along an unfamiliar country road or enjoyed a stroll through a quiet neighbourhood, you have probably seen them. A birdhouse in the shape of a stately mansion, a weather vane depicting two lumberjacks sawing wood, a scarecrow made in the image of a Mountie.

Quaint, often handmade items that people might invent to either pass the time, decorate their surroundings or show their sense of humour. Although not necessarily the intent when they were created, these expressions said something about the times, the culture and the people who created them. Something uniquely Canadian.

For more than seventy years, the Canadian Museum of Civilization has collected these expressions of our country's history in the form of traditional folk art. These pieces, gathered from all parts of Canada, reflect the everyday way of life of the people who built and gave character to this country.

Investors Group as well has a seventy-year history of helping Canadians reach their financial goals and aspirations. We are proud to partner with the Museum in sponsoring the exhibition and national tour of *This Other Eden: Canadian Folk Art Outdoors*—the largest cultural sponsorship in our company's history. Our involvement with this project underlines the support Investors Group provides for arts and culture in Canada. It also reflects our support for the Canadian Museum of Civilization and the way this fine institution preserves and shares the special aspects of our Canadian heritage.

At Investors Group, we believe we have a responsibility to contribute to the quality of life in the communities in which we live and work. That is why we are so pleased to help bring this distinctive exhibition to centres across Canada as part of our ongoing commitment to sharing culture with Canadians.

H. SANFORD RILEY
President and C.E.O.
Investors Group Inc.

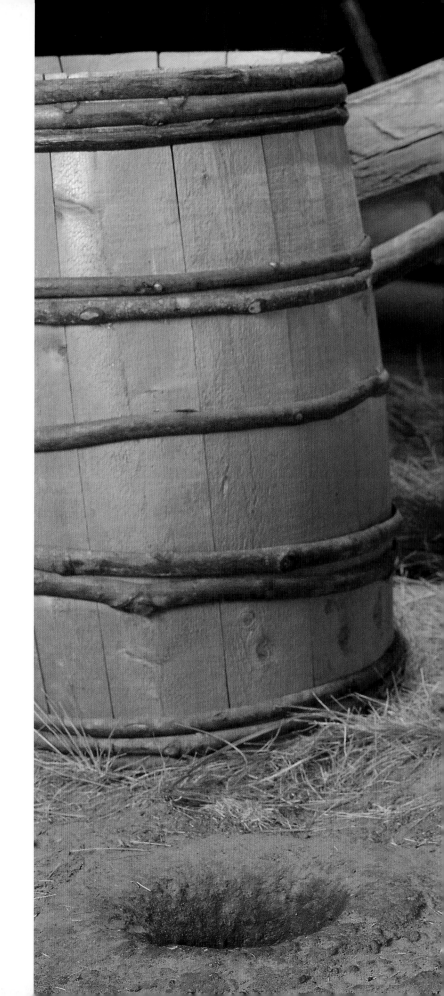

4

An anonymous cow waits benignly
for milking time. (Harry Foster;
CMC 76-463)

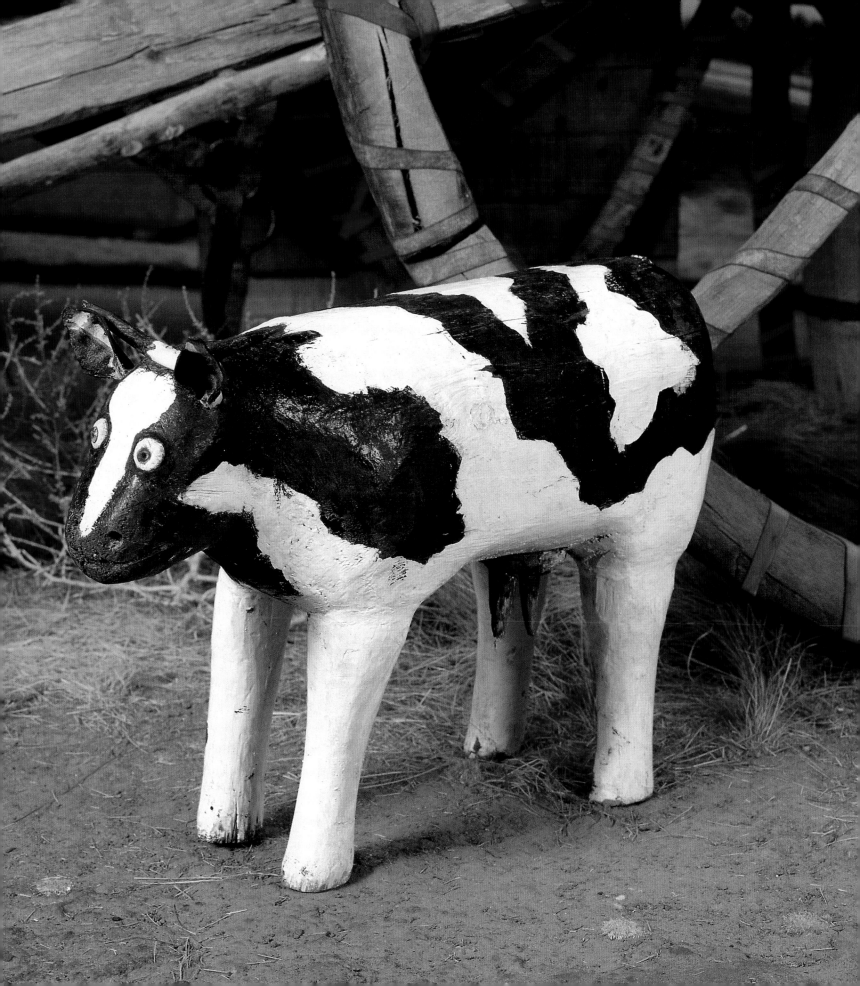

A Vast Landscape Writ Small

ONCE DISMISSED AS PRIMITIVE or naïve, Canadian folk art has long since achieved the respect it so richly deserves. The outdoor folk art pieces you will see in this book pre-date the mass-produced lawn and garden ornaments of today and stand as monuments to the originality of generations of Canadian folk artists. From elaborate whirligigs and witty automata to lawn sculpture of stark and simple beauty, the pieces in *This Other Eden: Canadian Folk Art Outdoors* are sure to delight even the most casual observer.

Folk art is perhaps the most democratic art form there is, for it is driven purely by the personal taste of its creators. And therein lies its vitality—for an art that cares little for the opinion of the world beyond its front gate is free to give full rein to whatever form of expression it chooses. Folk art is, in essence, an untutored inspiration—one in which ordinary people express their creativity and imagination in many different ways. Ironically, it also ends in being the most universal. Few of us seeing the proud adornment of a weathered birdhouse or a flying Canada goose on someone's front lawn will not respond with nostalgia, amusement or a smile of recognition. Perhaps more than any other art form in Canada, folk art also evokes who we are as a nation: who we are in response to a vast, open landscape that drives us to personalize and demystify our own small corner of the world.

The works in this book and its companion exhibition were drawn from the Canadian Museum of Civilization's extensive folk art collections, curated by Phil Tilney. However, the exhibition and this book would not have been possible without the generous support of Investors Group Inc. and particularly of Richard Irish. We are proud to have Investors Group as our partner in this project and are pleased to attach ourselves to an organization with such a long-standing commitment to the visual and performing arts in Canada. Dedicated—as are we—to showcasing Canadian heritage coast to coast, Investors Group has made it possible for us to reach out to all Canadians, from those who have never seen a whirligig in their lives to those who adore the witty, cranky and eccentric appeal of Canada's rich folk art traditions.

ADRIENNE CLARKSON
Chairwoman, Board of Directors
Canadian Museum of Civilization

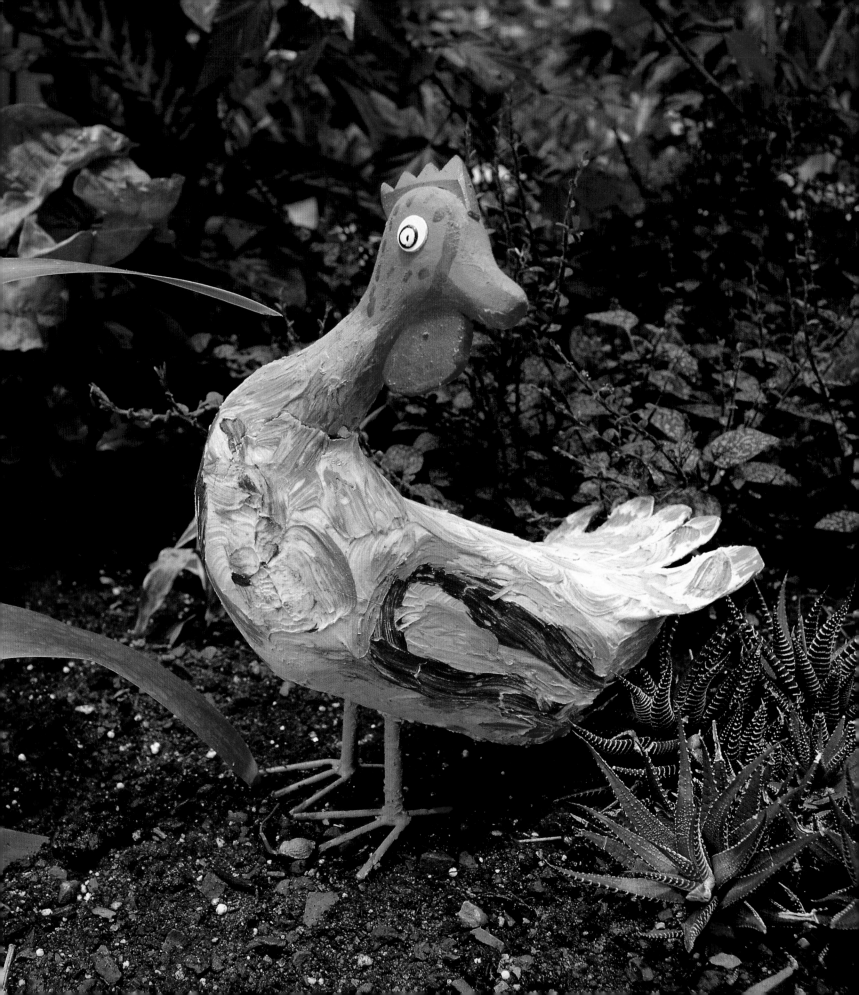

Foreword by Bill Richardson

I THINK I WAS IN HIGH SCHOOL before I had acquired enough information to understand that all the streets in our subdivision were called after adventurers. Palliser and Hind and Kane were among the asphalt memorials to a few of the brave but relatively unremarked worthies who had paddled the nearby rivers and strode through the tall grasses that once laid claim to our Winnipeg neighbourhood. My brothers and I grew up on Hearne, which was named in honour of Samuel Hearne, an English explorer who in the 1770s undertook an arduous trek through what would become the northern territories of Canada, and whose journals are full of fantastic and sometimes bloody stories. Hearne was intrepid and restless. He probably would have been disappointed to know that his name would one day be conjoined with so safe and often-trod a route as is his namesake avenue.

At the corner where Hearne met Lodge was a ranch-style house with a big back yard. When we were boys—which was when winters were colder than they are now, and when there was still a tall but delicate weeping birch casting its summertime shade across the bend of the road—the big back yard of the

Facing page: This ebullient chicken is the handiwork of Quebec artist Félicien Lévesque. Chickens are one of the most frequently depicted barnyard creatures, appearing in folk art paintings and hooked rugs, on weather vanes and as outdoor statuary. (Harry Foster; CMC 90-283)

ranch-style house was enclosed by a rustic log fence. At first glance, it made the lot—which was in every other way conventional—look rather like a corral, which after all meshed with the idea of "ranch." Atop the roof was another countrifying touch, and that was a weather vane. This useful ornament, made of iron, I imagine, or maybe of tin, was cast in the shape of a rooster. The rooster's head was raised in a dawn-time posture of crowing, and the bird balanced expertly upon a crossbar, the four points of which were capped with moulded letters: N, S, E and W.

Every morning, at least during the summer months, my younger brother and I would walk to the corner, look up and study the rooster to see from which direction the wind was blowing. Sometimes, the rooster would be so firmly and fixedly aligned with a cardinal point that the reading would be unequivocal. Sometimes, it conveyed a more ambivalent message. On such days as these, we would have the pleasure of nodding to one another and saying, "Ah! North by northwest." Or, "South by southeast." It has never occurred to me until now to wonder just why we folded such intelligence gathering into our routine. Neither of us was clever enough to study the rooster and think of saying, "Looks like fowl weather," and our devotion surely had nothing whatsoever to do with vocational aspiration. True, we had a second cousin whom we called Uncle and who was a government meteorologist, but as he lived in distant Ottawa and as he rarely visited and as he never talked about his work in a way that might encourage emulation or jog us along a career path, I think we can safely discount his influence in this regard. I can't recall that we were outstandingly interested in other manifestations of the weather. We paid the thermometer little mind. We kept no rain gauges. We didn't measure snow drifts. There was only the summertime meander down to where Hearne met Lodge to check out the morning mind of the rooster.

In fact, now that I think of it, weather had not much to do with the acting out of our odd matinal ritual. Had we been interested in the simple fact of the wind and its prevailing direction, it would have been easy enough to look at the sky and note the path taken by high-flying cumulus puffs or to read the register of the passing air in the leaves of the trees. It would have been easy enough to wet a finger and hold it aloft. The wind figured only insofar as it had made necessary the weather vane, which was the only one anywhere around, and which delighted us. It was fanciful. In a way, it made us hopeful. That rooster, with its divided directional loyalties, connected us, albeit at a subconscious level, with the certainty that while Hearne Avenue might be our beginning it was not necessarily our end; that while Hearne was nothing but a fixed freckle on the face of the planet, west and east and south and north went on forever, circling the globe, wrapping it in colourful meridians. An ordinary weather vane, perhaps given as a gift, perhaps purchased on a whim, and probably attached to the peak of the roof by a do-it-yourself kind of husband while his wife watched and fretted from below—we are talking the '50s, after all—did what all art, great or minor, should do. It took us out of ourselves. It linked us to something that was beyond. Only connect. Only connect. At a distance, but in a real way, and via the vane, we did.

One of the many intriguing details Phil Tilney has in his arsenal and that he lets fly to wonderful effect in *This Other Eden* is the theory that the classic rooster weather vane, once a fanciful staple of church tops, was said to have its origins in the story of how St. Peter betrayed Jesus three times before cockcrow. Those who make it their business to question the veracity of such lore think this thesis is without foundation, which is too bad since it is so charming. Frankly, I'd be hesitant to dismiss it out of hand. Some of the latter-day perfidies that have attached themselves to garden folk art make one wonder if there isn't something about the stuff that invites treachery, just as it invites thoughts of elsewhere. Every several months, it seems, the papers will give over a few column inches to yet another wacky news item (what they call in the trade "brights") about garden art that has fallen prey to felons. Typically, these stories involve some sort of kitschy lawn ornament—a gnome, a frog, a minor Disney character such as one of the seven dwarves, perhaps a Virgin or some other saintly grotto dweller—that is stolen away under cover of night and taken on a trip to far-flung places. The perpetrators of these crimes rub salt in the wounds of the bereaved by sending back photographs of the abducted tchotchke, taken at a café in Paris, or in an Istanbul market, or at Mount Rushmore. Eventually, the unwitting prodigal returns to its lawn of origin, a repatriation that happens with little or no ceremony. One morning the sun rises, and lo and behold it is back. Someone calls the local paper. A photographer comes by and the image hits the wire service and everyone has a good chuckle and then forgets about it till it happens again.

Reports of such occurrences make me nervous. They remind me of the vulnerability to theft of a sturdy example of garden art that is one of our treasured family heirlooms. The piece in question was crafted by my father— a talented woodcarver in the folk tradition—almost twenty-five years ago. It's a life-size statue of our family dog, a springer spaniel called Mitch. The shape of the sitting Mitch was liberated from a stump that was left in our yard on Hearne Avenue after a tall oak tree sickened and had to be cut down. Unlike most garden statuary, which is reasonably portable, Mitch would require a considerable effort of will and some mechanical intervention to be removed, since he is quite literally rooted to the ground. Nonetheless, I have to believe that if delinquents will go to the lengths of hauling a garden-variety garden gnome all the way to Melbourne and back, they might just be primed to take up a chainsaw and see to the brazen broad-daylight removal of a one-of-a-kind prize such as Mitch, who has become one of the neighbourhood constants. He is unwavering in his posture or regard, save that come wintertime his fond maker and guardian always crowns him with a woolly tuque.

My parents have been in that house for more than forty years. Eventually, no doubt, and sooner rather than later, they will choose to leave it. Come that day, they will have to decide whether to number Mitch among their portable chattels, or whether to leave him to the care and tender mercies of whatever family comes along next. Much as I would hate to see him pass from the family fold, I rather hope he remains behind; hope even more that the new occupants keep him as a sentinel and honour his long-standing contract with the life of the street.

Why should I care? I have not lived there for more than twenty years, never will live there again. But I continue to visit several times a year, and when I go for walks down Hearne, I steer myself in the direction of Lodge. As I pass the ranch-style house at the corner, I look reflexively up to the roof to get an answer about the wind. I look up half-harbouring the hope that someone will have replaced the rooster weather vane, which has been gone for years and years. On such occasions as these, I miss the easy commerce I had with the great anodyne of fantasy when I was a child. Then, I could have found succour and reassurance in believing that it had fallen under a Chagallesque enchantment, had spread its tinny wings and flown the coop for Roosterland, or that it had been hijacked by brigands from Bremen and would one day make its way back to its habitual roost. But maturation strips us of such possibilities and leaves only the prosaic likelihood that it fell prey to the bland depredations of time and weather, or to something as commonplace and necessary as a household move. Of course, it is a minor absence, but I do miss it. I do. And I like to think that one of the children who now lives on the street, or who walks along it towards the nearby school, pays Mitch the same sort of mind we paid the weather vane. I like to think that Mitch, who is not nearly so useful, whose only functions are to cast a shadow and to delight, will be there years hence when that child, following whatever agenda, returns to Hearne, trailing clouds of experience and sadness. I like to think that Mitch will be there still, a souvenir of something that is almost innocent; that he will remain, long-eared and mossy, but an angel nonetheless, quietly guarding the gate that leads to a private, minor Eden.

Acknowledgements

MANY THANKS TO the curatorial gang in a previous life at the National Museum of Man who trained me, prodded me, kidded me and let me go: Bob Klymasz, Magnús Einarsson, Paul Carpentier, Wes Mattie, Pierre Crépeau and Bill Taylor, who pushed folk art behind the scenes.

Thanks today to the Canadian Museum of Civilization's crack last-minute exhibition team of Danielle Goyer, Pam Cross, Isabel Jones, Anne Malépart and designer Amber Walpole, who all picked up the ball and ran with it. Mind you, without Sylvie Morel, Stephen Inglis and George MacDonald, there would have been no game. And without Wes Mattie, again, and Harry Foster, there would have been no photographs. Many thanks to the Governor-General's Greenhouse, Government House, the Ottawa Experimental Farm Tropical Greenhouse, and the Canadian Museum of Civilization's Canada Hall for allowing us to take location photographs.

Finally, thanks to Ellen Tilney, Andrée Juneau and Ann Milovsoroff of the Royal Botanical Gardens in Hamilton, whose gardening expertise and enthusiasm got me off the ground, and knee-deep in compost, so to speak.

PHIL TILNEY
Guest Curator, *This Other Eden: Canadian Folk Art Outdoors*

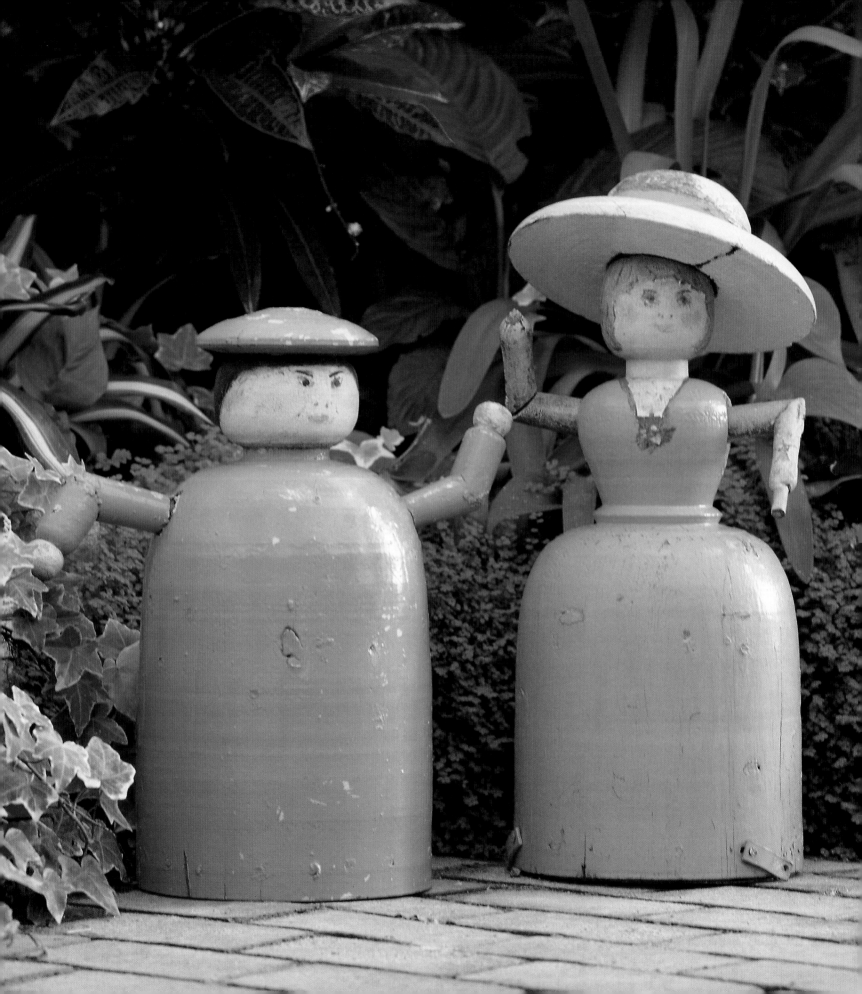

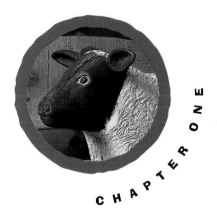

CHAPTER ONE

Folk Art in the Garden: Today and Yesterday

WE'VE ALL SEEN IT, the cheerful yard that is the latest incarnation of outdoor folk art. Once we start looking for it, we see it even more often.

There is the painstakingly clipped rural or suburban front lawn, then the swept and tended laneway, and the careful flower plantings. Suddenly, the pair of painted gnomes beneath the yew bush under the front window comes into focus—just behind the puffy and fully gowned Bo-Peep, tending her single, Dynel sheep; not far from the pair of faded, pink plastic flamingoes. One is standing stiffly at attention, the other is bending over, pretending to feed.

The man with the distinctly Asian face and the woman in Victorian dress are birdhouses that sat on adjoining fence posts in Cornwall, Ontario. Their entrances are at the back. (Harry Foster; CMC 78-590 [1,2,3])

In the middle of the yard is a cultured island of petunias, pink, white and purple, surrounding the shingled wooden wishing well. And at the base, a mother duck is pursued by several yellow hatchlings, all waddling towards the house. At the right is a silhouette, a pair actually, a black cut-out dog chasing a cat. And yes, near the flowers at the side of the property, a Granny Fanny, the brightly painted jigsaw sculpture of a generously proportioned woman bending over. Blue jeans, red handkerchief and patterned stockings.

Across the laneway, a wooden bucket lies on its side, giving the cornucopia impression that the tumble of marigolds in front of it have poured from its interior. Regarding this remarkable illusion are two wooden bunnies, a surprised pink pig and a solemn green frog. They also look towards an articulated figure of Tweetie Bird planted near the road, whose feet turn slowly in the lazy breeze. A matching, colourful Tweetie flag printed with the phrase "Home Tweet Home" flaps gently near the front door.

This is the "faux folk art" of the Canadian outdoors, continuing a tradition of yard and garden decoration that has developed over thousands of years. Of course it is not "folk" art in any of the classic senses; hardly a single piece is handmade, and store-bought items predominate. True folk art was the tangible artistic expression of ordinary, unschooled people who wished to manifest their aesthetic impulses in carving, painting, textiles, assemblage—an amazing variety of media. Early folk art was very demanding; it had to be done exactly according to tradition. Just right, in other words. It was symbolic, community art that demonstrated the skill of the maker, and was a personal accomplishment, completed with care, thought, memory and often sly, even ribald humour.

This is particularly true of work by those artists who chose to exhibit their creations outdoors, drawing the eye and the attention of passers-by.

Statuary and artistic interpretations of one sort or another have graced outdoor living spaces since humankind first settled in a single spot. Ancient Egypt had carved and decorated gateposts; Roman gardens were filled with stone sculptures, some astonishingly naughty; and from the Renaissance on, enclosed gardens boasted artworks of a remarkable variety. Although in some cases mounted for reasons other than pure decoration, the carved house posts and free-standing totem poles of Canada's native peoples are part of a time-honoured tradition. In much of the rest of Canada, decorative weather vanes have been a fact of rural life for more than a century, but their artistic or religious aspects were undoubtedly secondary to their forecasting, and thus useful, capabilities.

In rural and suburban Canada, lawn and garden decoration is a rather more recent phenomenon. Although lawns were nominally invented in the eighteenth century—yes, someone actually had to design them—they were not a common sight on this side of the Atlantic until the beginning of the twentieth century. In both Upper and Lower Canadian cities and settlements, houses were built close to the street, sometimes too close to allow for a garden, much less any decorative elements on the ground. In more roomy situations, any extra space was usually allotted to herb and vegetable growing, again the useful taking precedence over the purely artistic. After the Second World War, however, when the suburbs became a fact of life, front yard space evolved into what we have come to believe is the historical norm.

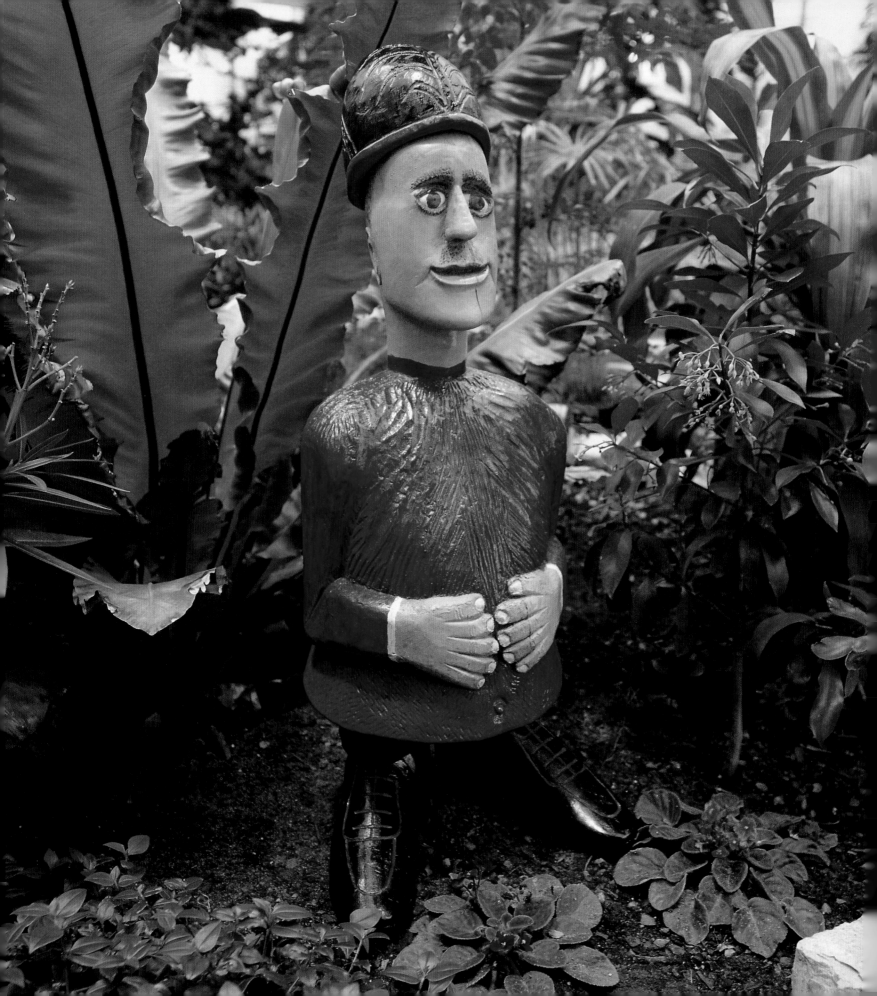

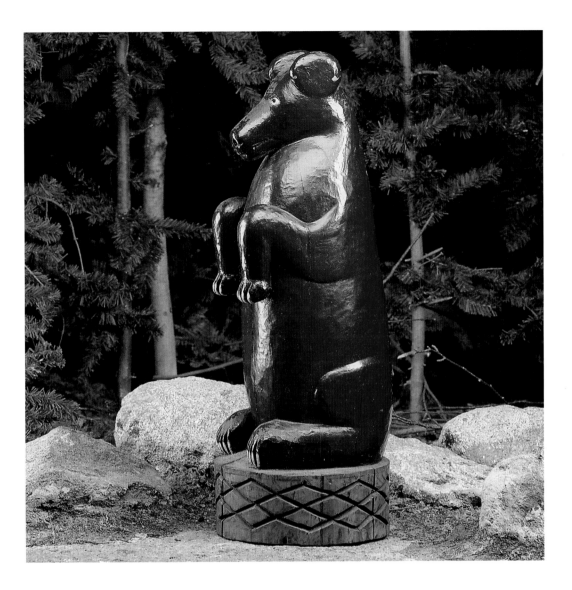

This may be the kindest, most appealing bear in the national collections. J. Seton Tompkins of Singhampton, Ontario, filled his yard with a series of remarkable carvings, including this bear, reminiscent of a hungry Labrador retriever. (Harry Foster; CMC 79-1839)

Facing page: Ti-Gus stood on a tiny island in Rosaire Leblanc's farm pond in Sainte-Sophie-de-Lévard, Quebec. Ti is short for *petit,* a nickname usually reserved for children or characters held in special regard. M. Leblanc made Ti-Gus to amuse his grandchildren and created a whole world of carved figures on the island, including a tiny house to which Ti-Gus moved for the winter. (Harry Foster; CMC 76-473)

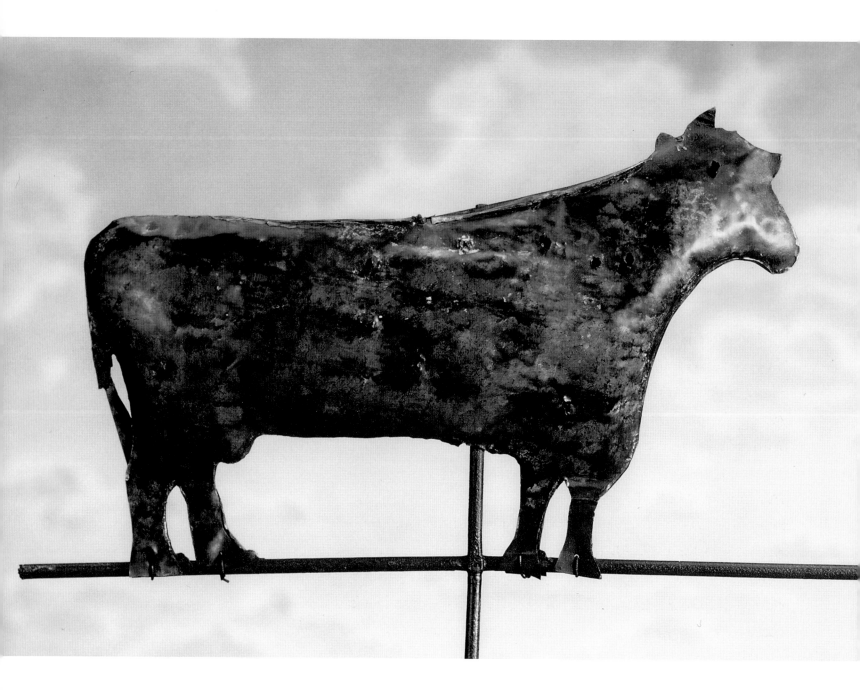

This severe bull stood atop a barn in Saint-Julie-de-Verchères, Quebec. Note the myriad bullet holes. Weather vanes were and undoubtedly still are a favourite target for hunters and country sharpshooters. (Harry Foster; CMC 71-301)

At first, properly trimmed lawngrass was the single most important fact of the postwar front yard. Kentucky bluegrass became a North American staple grass plant, even though it originally came from Europe or possibly the Middle East. The Canadian lawn represented a separation from the street, a statement, perhaps, that the owner had enough money for a free-standing house and a space at its front that did not, in fact, have to be used for anything, except to silently proclaim a certain status. Social gatherings, cookouts, birthday parties and other hilarity took place in the back yard, not on the front lawn. As other writers have pointed out, there was also an immediate (or possibly continuing) tradition of no fences on the front lawn, making all the lawns on a street into a single, cooperative, conformity-inducing space.

But into this quasi-formal space marched the persons scholars have dubbed "the folk." Plain grass was not enough. Flowers as ornaments appeared, also neatly tended, but these were not enough either. So at last appeared folk art specifically made for outdoors, created in the soul yet placed in the garden. It is these objects that we celebrate in this discussion.

The Rise and Fall of Outdoor Folk Art

From the 1960s on, leisure time was suddenly more important than it ever had been. Making and placing handmade objects in the front yard became increasingly common. The gardens of Westmount, Rosedale or Shaughnessy Heights did not suddenly sprout whirligigs, birdhouses and chainsaw statues of bears, but in rural Canada and distant suburbia, such adornments swiftly became the norm.

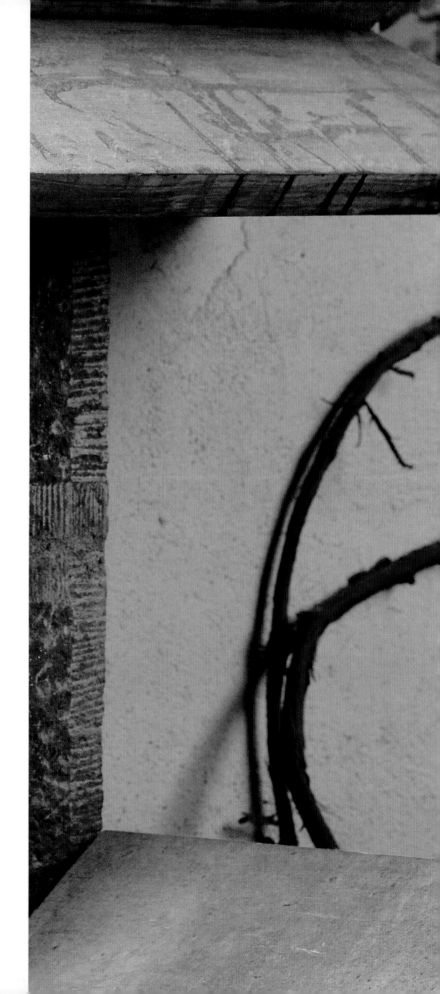

An inscrutable Collins Eisenhauer
cat calmly observes a world
only it can fully understand. (Harry
Foster; CMC 76-387)

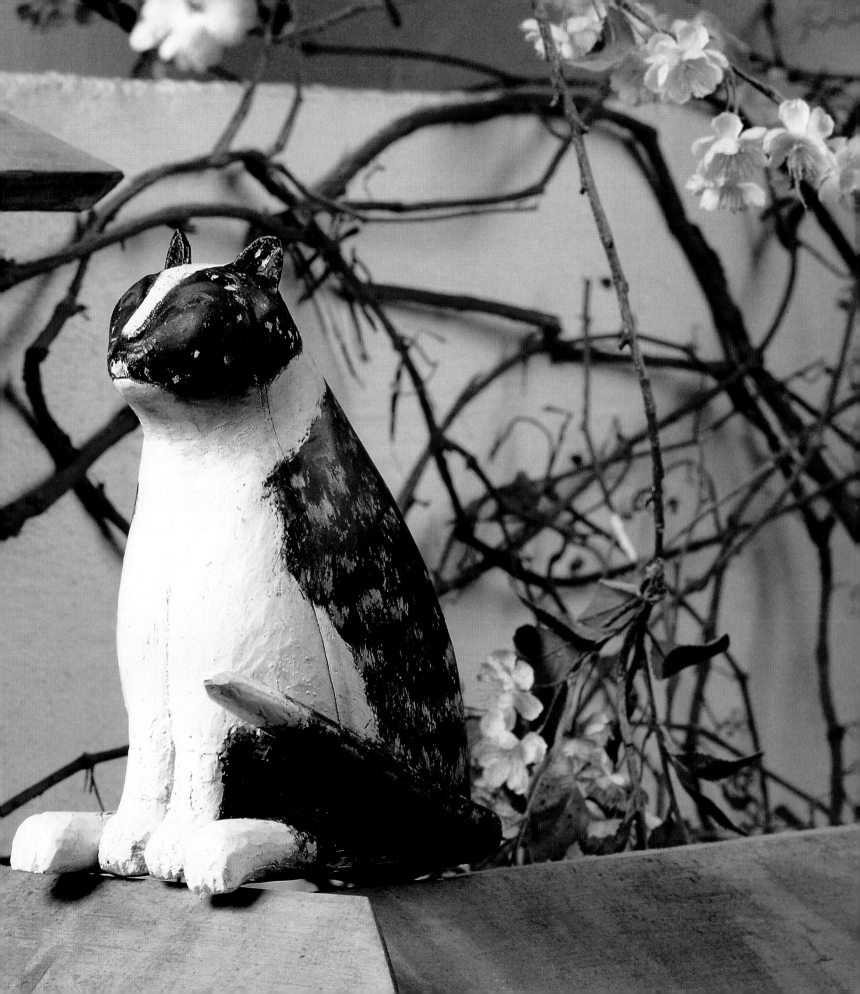

For three decades, talented folk creators in the Atlantic provinces made myriad seagull whirligigs and coast-related statuary for placement between the house and the road. In Quebec, home-grown sculptors created fantasy gardens filled with painted rocks and edgy creations, a more personal folk art that came to be called the *patenteux* tradition. In Ontario and across the prairies, "naïve" folk sculptors, painters and inventors of every sort—all totally untrained in the arts—lavished their attentions on mailboxes, barn doors and bird decoys, often using their immigrant-based decoration techniques to finish their works. And on the Pacific coast, "unconscious" folk sculptors, whose motivation was merely to decorate their living spaces, also worked in much the same rich practices of outdoor art, although their work was eclipsed some-

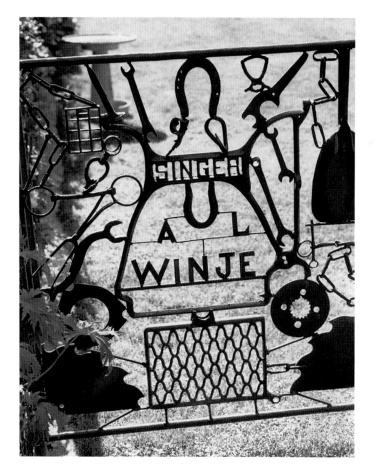

what by the pervasive Native traditions already so entrenched in the popular imagination.

Most contemporary folk art was completed without any audience in mind, an isolated, just-for-myself art, but some folk artists revelled in the attention their work brought them. During this extraordinarily productive period, collectors, art dealers and pickers for museums and galleries became very interested in folk art creations. Here was a commercial venture too good to be missed. In some cases they did not know quite what it was they were collecting, but they knew it would sell—sometimes for enormous prices.

Others—anathema to museum researchers—hid all but the names of their artists, hoping to become their exclusive agents, but at the same time concealing, losing or not caring about the importance of contextual information so essential to the next generation of scholars. Antique dealers bought and bargained, museum curators bought and preserved, and collectors celebrated the pieces that hung on their walls and over their fireplaces. Single duck decoys, one of the most obvious outdoor folk pieces, became the darlings of interior decorators, and their prices rose from single digits to hundreds of thousands of dollars apiece in art auctions run by the elite.

But suddenly, in the 1990s the bubble burst. Two things happened. First—and most important—the folk artists stopped producing. All that amazing creative frenzy, essentially the product of a pre-technical, rural age, had ended. Making money became more important; people suddenly seemed to have less time. Very simply, lawn decorations that once were made at home could be bought in a shop.

Second, buying and selling homemade pieces was no longer a money-making proposition. "No one," as one canny gallery owner was heard to say, "is naïve any more." Oh, a few pieces were still being made in isolated workshops, but as the commercial rewards diminished, the quality declined precipitously. By the mid 1990s, it was almost impossible to find a genuine "folk" artist, just as it was almost impossible to find a gallery with genuine, unconsciously artistic and newly minted "folk" materials.

The Canadian Museum of Civilization and others lucky enough to have acquired some of this genuine folk material abruptly found themselves

Facing page: Albert Winje made remarkable folk statuary from masses of recycled metal. This is his front gate, made from sewing-machine parts, tools, chains and horse-bridle hardware. Slocan City, British Columbia. (Wes Mattie)

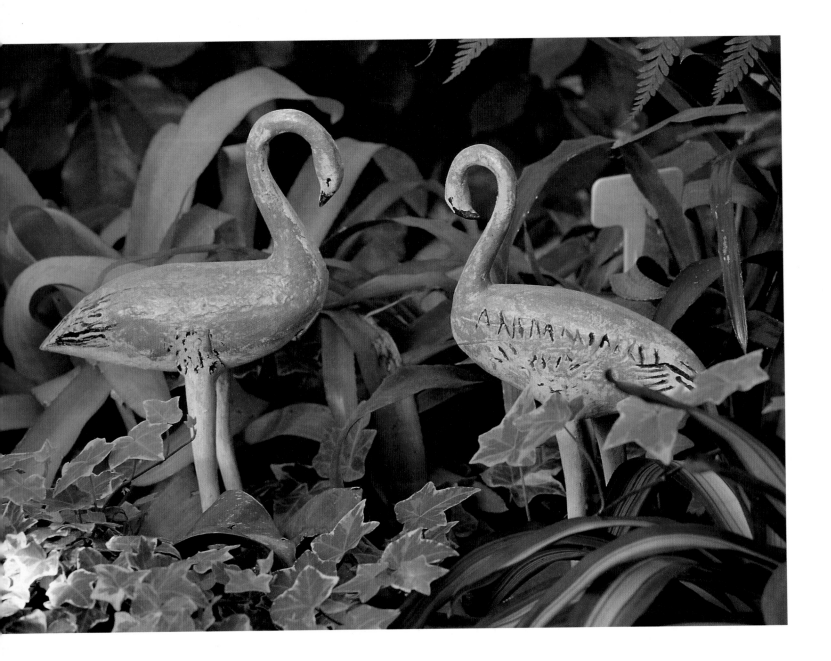

Pink flamingoes in the Canadian garden have a surprisingly long history. This pair of wooden birds was carved by John Hummel, a well-known Maryhill, Ontario, Mennonite carver who worked mostly in the 1940s. Plastic pink flamingoes remain the quintessential staple of the decorated front yard. (Harry Foster; CMC 77-740, 77-741)

Facing page: A French Canadian frog of unassailable dignity. (Harry Foster; CMC 81-136)

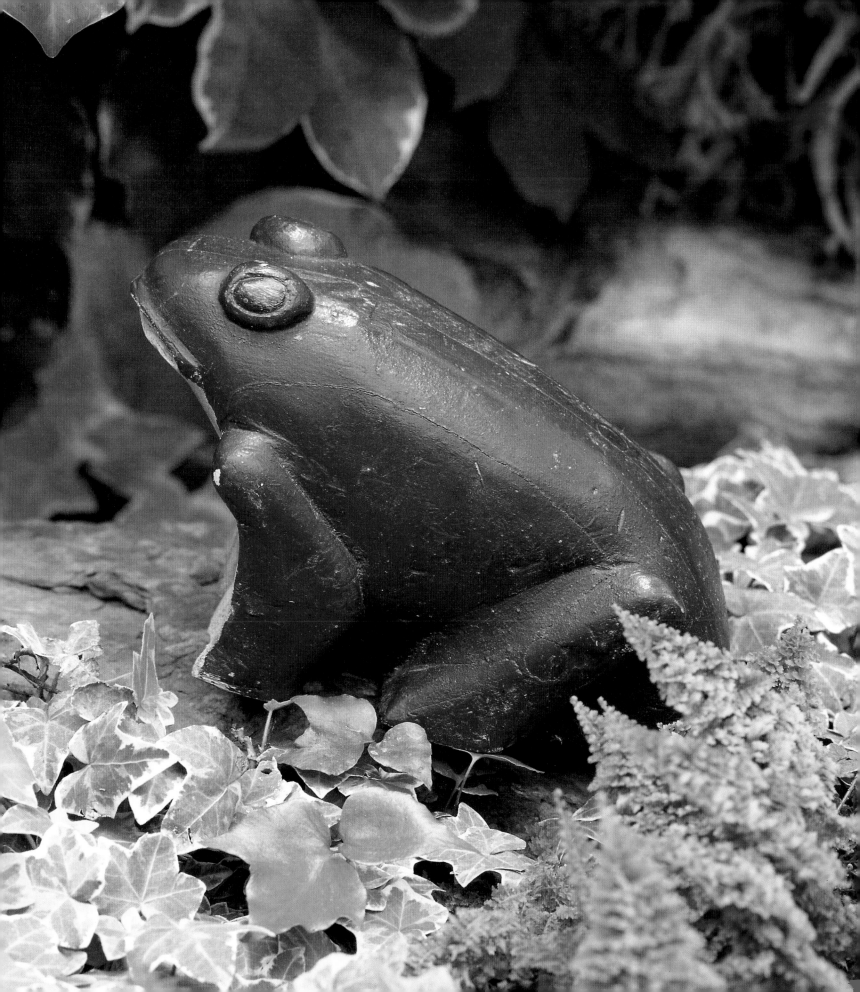

with significant folk culture collections. In essence, the outdoor folk art collections, as a whole, had become rather valuable artifacts almost overnight. Museums, charged with protection and preservation of cultural materials that bespeak a decade, a generation or, in this case, a specific artistic period, were instant repositories and protectors of an age that had just passed. It was a unique position to find themselves in. Once accused in some quarters as collectors of "yard junk," they were now suddenly defenders of a large portion of important material culture, the sources of which had unexpectedly dried up.

One cannot help but think in terms of the lucky museum that at the turn of the century found itself with the definitive collection of buggy whips. When overnight, buggy whips were no longer required, made or sold, the definitive museum buggy whip collection would have assumed more importance than anyone might have guessed.

How the Folk Are Always One Step Ahead

The true bearers of folk culture always seem to be at least one step in front of their interpreters. Those who created all the magnificent folk sculpture of the '70s and '80s had now moved on to other concerns. They continued to decorate their front gardens, but like the rest of the continent, they looked to others to provide the items they had been providing themselves. In short, they turned to commercial and what we might term "semi-commercial" outlets for material to decorate their front yards.

Shops carrying "country" or indeed "folklore" articles began to appear, many of them actually selling small statuary to put on the lawn. Producers who had never really stopped making birdbaths and other cast-concrete objects found that business was better than ever.

In addition, a few semi-commercial hobbyists responded to this vacuum, fired up their jigsaws and created a further wild variety of birdhouses, whirligigs and lawn figures. Interestingly enough, these were not, for the most part, former folk artists. They were basement hobbyists who were following newly published pattern books on how to make, decorate and even what to charge for a whirligig. The market was there, and these jigsaw sculptors were ready to fill in.

The artists of outdoor art had essentially dropped out. However, this did not mean that decoration of the space in front of home was ignored. The desire to fill the garden with personal statements was still very much alive— *because the garden was still there.* The garden had been the background and context of the entire thirty years of the true folk art movement, and it would continue to be important in this new phase. The context had remained, even though the art faded away.

Subsequent chapters will address the meanings of folk art and its place within our society; specifically examine outdoor folk art; and parse the significance of the garden and gardening in its international and Canadian context. With this understanding of folk art and its environments, we will be in a better position to look into the future of Canadian folk art outdoors.

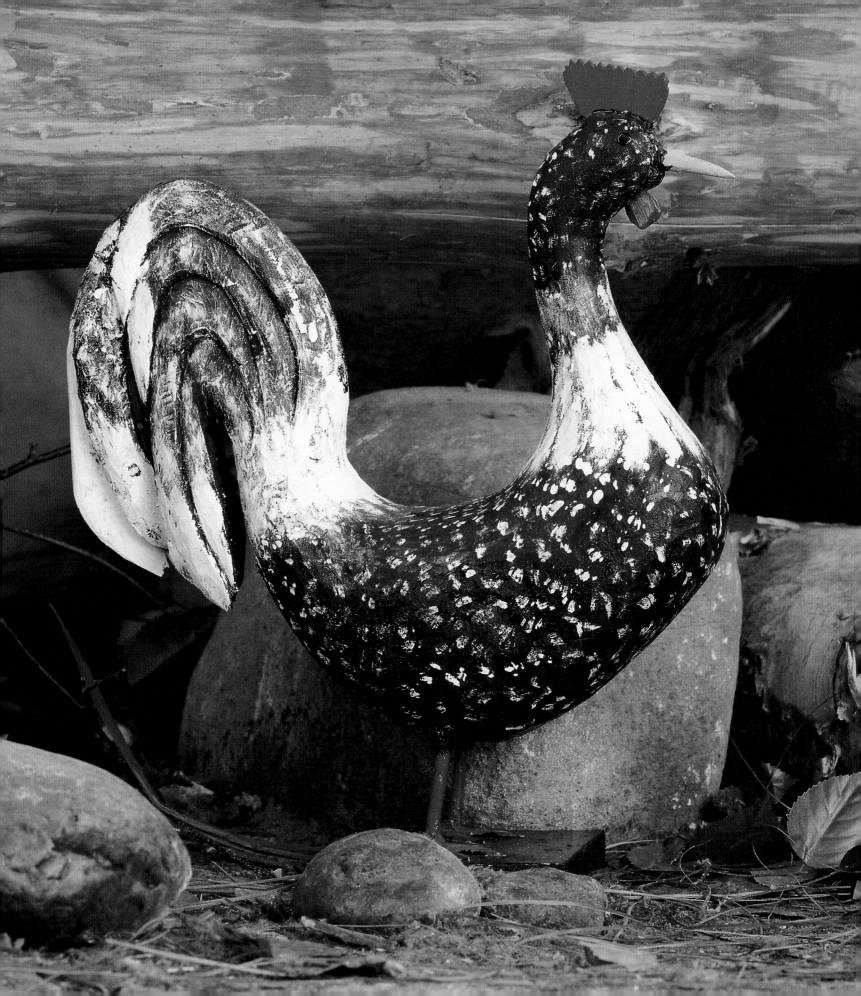

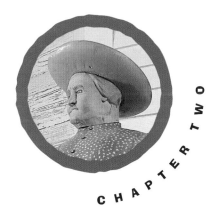

Folklore and Folk Art: Indoors and Out

THERE ARE TWO DIFFICULTIES when it comes to discussing folk art. One is the word "folk," and the other is the word "art." Both terms are so fraught with hideous and contentious issues that most people choose to ignore the intricacies of the phrase entirely and operate on a You-Know-What-I-Mean principle. This is without a doubt the best way to proceed.

Come to think about it, folk art is very much like the term "pornography" as defined by a United States Supreme Court justice back when there was some suspicion that *Lady Chatterly's Lover* might actually be literature and not

This dignified monarch of the barnyard was one of many splendid outdoor animal carvings by the multitalented Collins Eisenhauer of Union Square, Nova Scotia. (Harry Foster; CMC 77-385)

simply smut. "I can't really define pornography," he is reported to have said, "but I know it when I see it." In short, for "pornography" substitute "folk art," and we're there.

However, academics, former academics and curators, ahem, can't bear to leave this alone. Having even once attempted to explain the nature of folklore, the urge never dies. So hold on to your tuques. To gain an understanding of the term "folk," let's look at the general term "folklore," and then at "folk art."

What Is Folklore, Anyway?

Before folklorists were invented (yes, Virginia, somebody had to invent folklorists, and many agree it was a rather stuffy English writer named William John Thoms, who coined the word "folk-lore" in 1846), most anthropologists and culture hunters disdained folklore as worthless peasant creations. Those early scholars were interested in "primitive" arts and culture, "savage" myths and village artifacts such as digging sticks, weapons and talismans. It took pioneers like the Brothers Grimm to give traditional peasant "products" a good name.

Folklore, in fact, is the *traditional product of a folk group*. This definition is deceptively straightforward. First, it doesn't really define anything. Second, it leaves us with three additional terms to explain. Let's do one at a time.

"Traditional," the first term, means that something is produced in much the same way a number of times. The traditional teaching or transmission process is probably word of mouth. Traditions are usually not passed on in writing. If you're thinking folktales or folksongs, you're on the right track.

Originally, only oral products—not three-dimensional artifacts—were considered to be folklore. In addition, oral folklore is generally anonymous. If the "author" of a folktale were known, it might not count as a folktale at all.

Now let's take an artifact tradition, say quilt-making. Auntie Virtue makes quilts. She learned quilt-making from her mother, whose mother taught her, and so on; she's in the tradition. And her specialty is Double Wedding Ring Quilts. She's made lots of them. But is each one identical? No. As she's gotten older, the colours used have been slightly different, the materials in those circles have changed (she uses dacron instead of all cotton, possibly) and her hand stitches are never in exactly the same place. But still, every version is recognizable as a Double Wedding Ring Quilt in the quilting tradition.

The same principle can be applied to garden art. Weather vanes have been made by hand for about two thousand years. But since the time of Tutankhamen, weather vanes on the roof have pointed in the direction the wind is blowing. There are hundreds, possibly thousands of vane designs— arrows, animals, people, banners and so on—but they all do the same thing. They are a traditional wind-direction instrument, never identical, but made by a technology developed and handed down from generation to generation, probably by word of mouth. And they're even cross-cultural! Both Vikings and Quebec farmers made them, used them and decorated them. So even outdoor folk art has traditional aspects.

"Product" is the second element in the above definition of folklore, and a folk product can also be almost anything you might name that is "traditional." Historically, folklorists dealt with oral products: songs, stories, proverbs,

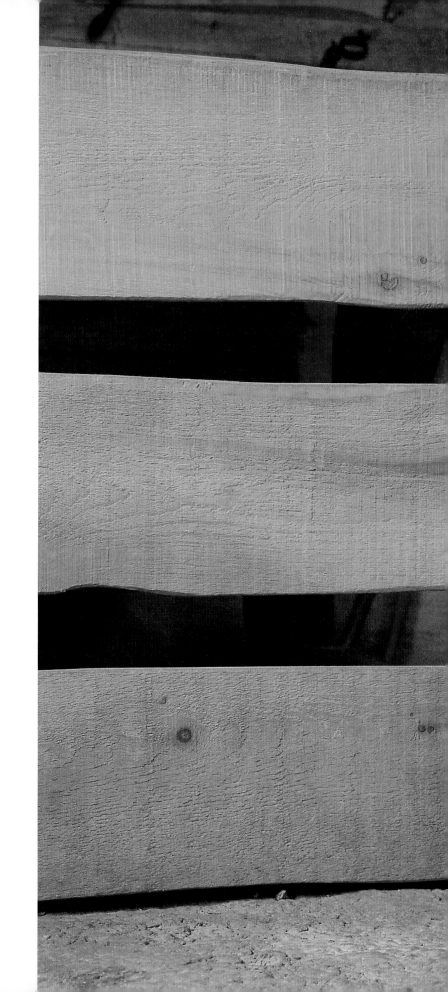

Billie Andrews was an orphaned English boy who came to work on a farm in Bradford, Ontario, after the First World War. He carved many of the creatures he saw on the farm, and this sheep was one of his special pets. (Harry Foster; CMC 76-486)

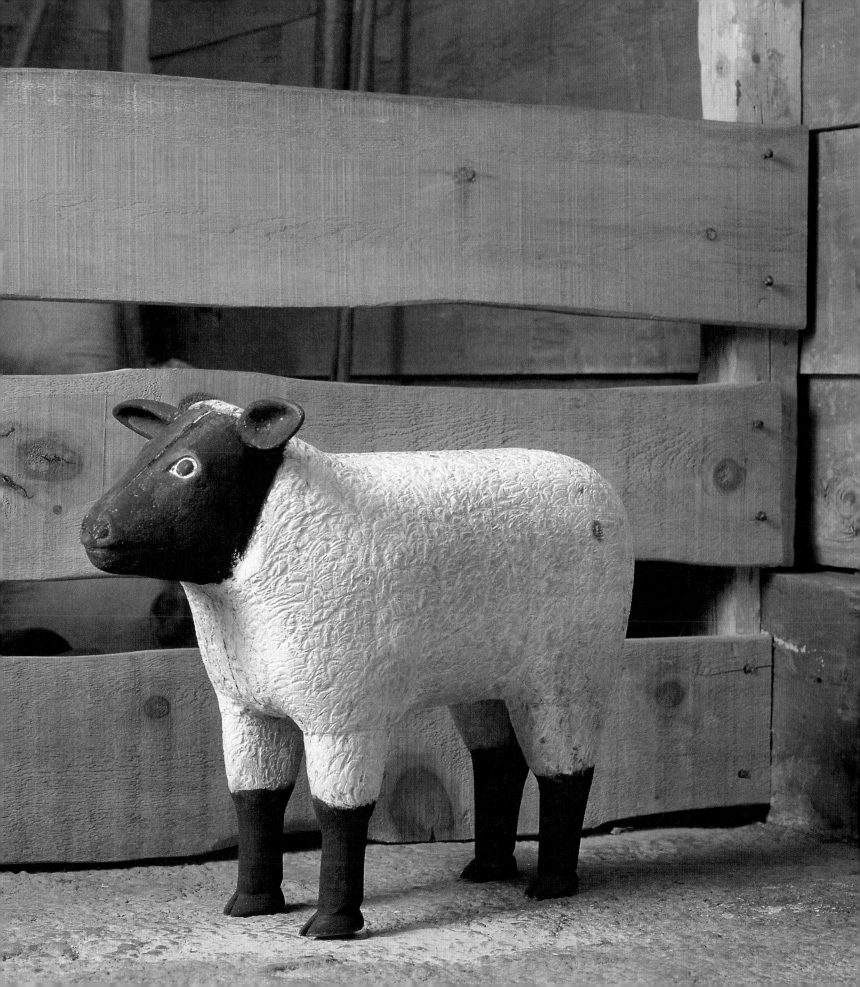

verbal lore of all sorts that was not necessarily written down, did not necessarily have a specific author, but which contained some nugget of wisdom valuable, funny or memorable enough to be passed on by word of mouth to the kids.

However, a folk product can be a three-dimensional object, in addition to a song or joke, such as Auntie Virtue's quilt and the pancultural weather vane. In the garden, there are also birdhouses, whirligig wind machines and a host of handmade decorations that are traditional and are also folk products.

Have your doubts about the historicity of whirligigs? At about the time the Chinese were inventing gunpowder, they also had garden wind machines, mostly in the form of chimes, but dependent on the motion of the wind nonetheless. Medieval and Renaissance Europeans had flags, banners and windsocks that entertained, identified and decorated; and well before Canada was Canada, lawn figures with whirling arms were well known, probably

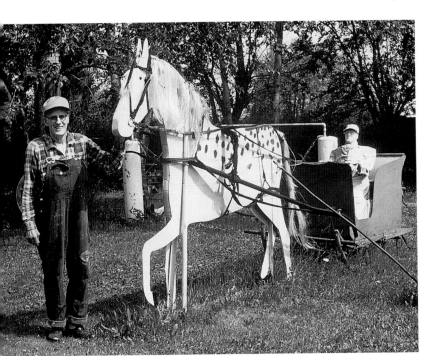

based on wind-driven pumps and grain grinders, which have been around for centuries. Renaissance Man Leonardo knew all about the propeller and the helicopter rotor, so whirli-machines were really nothing new. Kids played with hand-held pinwheels in the Middle Ages, the design based on wind-driven grain mills.

The modern-day whirligig, in fact, is a classic example of a traditional folk product.

The final element in the definition of folklore is "folk group." A folk group is made up of people who have something in common, often but not necessarily something traditional. It can be racially constituted, or based on similar education, profession, gender, age, size or even a particular skill, not to put too fine a point on any one of them. The former black slaves who came to Halifax on the Underground Railroad shared certain traditions as well as skin colour, and certainly became a Canadian folk group.

Blacksmiths, who share the same trade, all carry the same fairly esoteric knowledge and thus could be called a folk group. Prepubescent female agemates in Fiji one hundred years ago shared a variety of commonalities, and were undoubtedly a folk group.

The kids in Mrs. Brinley's grade five class know exactly when she will lose her temper, how she likes her reports handed in, and where on the desk everyone must keep their pencils. In this common and shared knowledge, Mrs. B's grade fives become a kind of folk group.

Canadians can be a folk group because they share special knowledge and behaviours, eh? And, of course, within Canada there are a great variety of folk groups, some based on nationality, language, dance, cuisine; in short, shared traditions of a large number of stripes help form and cement a folk group. One other point: people in those groups are "the folk." Folk artists, even though they do things not even remotely connected to other folk artists, might well be members of one or several folk groups. Think of yourself for a moment. Are you a member of one or more folk groups?

Facing page: Folk artists often try to recreate their memories of times gone by. Richard Adkins, of Westlock, Alberta, stands near the full-size horse silhouette and cutter he made for his yard. The passenger is probably a self-portrait. (Wes Mattie)

And so it is that an examination of folklore, the traditional product of a folk group, brings us at least part-way to folk art, the multifaceted aesthetic expressions produced by people without specific training who wish to tangibly express their creativity.

What Is Folk Art?

Any precise definition of art is open to question, so I'll avoid a Platonic discussion of serious Art (Truth and Beauty notwithstanding). I think that as is the case with the term pornography, we pretty well know what art is, even if we can't define it in ten words or less.

The same can be said of folk art. Folk art is one of those many "products" of folklore, and thus it is traditional and is often produced by one or more talented members of a folk group. But of course, there's more to it.

Folk art is usually something one step beyond the mundane. Not a container to bring water to the mouth for survival (cupped hands, for example), but a cup lovingly fashioned to bring pleasure or attract notice even when it is not being used to transport water. A nicely carved canoe cup is period folk art at its best.

Auntie Virtue could have just sandwiched some warm batting between two plain white sheets, but she chose instead to continue the tradition of piecing together interlocking, multicoloured rings because it pleased her and pleased whoever looked at them too. A simple art, not exactly a Rubens nude, mind you, but a "comfortable art," as the great textile historian

Facing page: Robert Campbell's clever whirligig is the quintessential farm scene of nature in revolt. Propelled by a unique arrangement of aluminum cups, the mechanics of this piece are reminiscent of the Javex-bottle whirligigs so common across the country. This comic piece stood in Mr. Campbell's yard in Gilbert Plains, Manitoba. (Harry Foster; CMC 70-60)

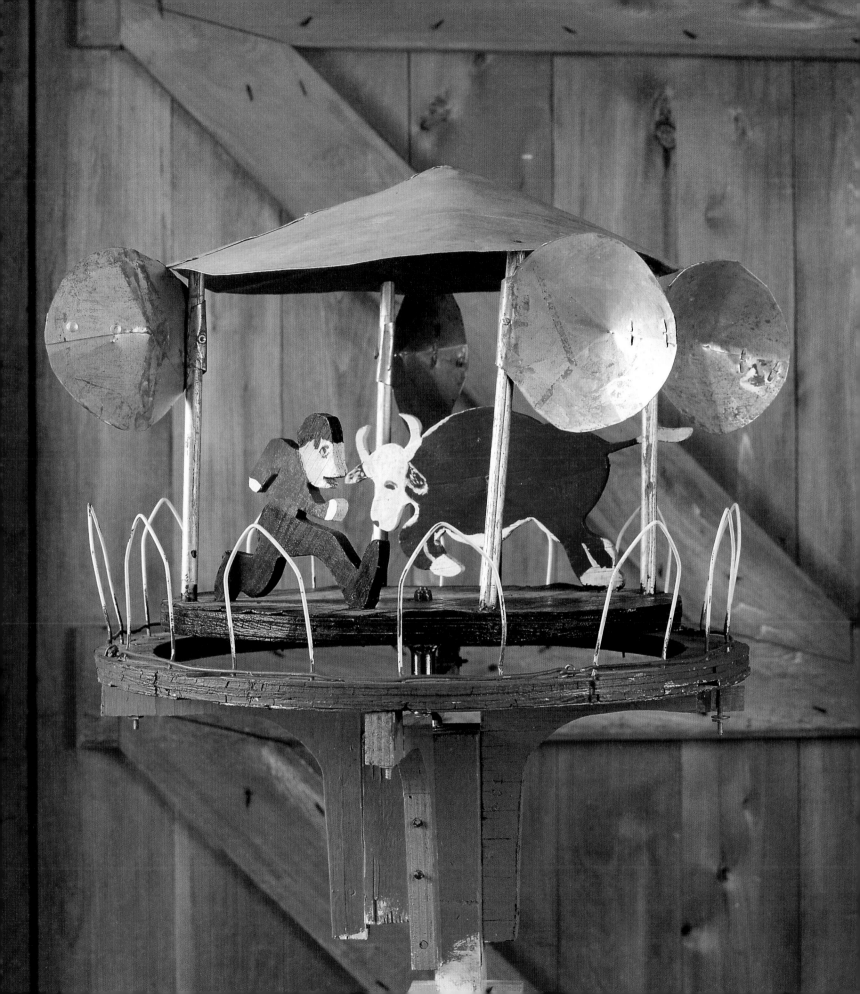

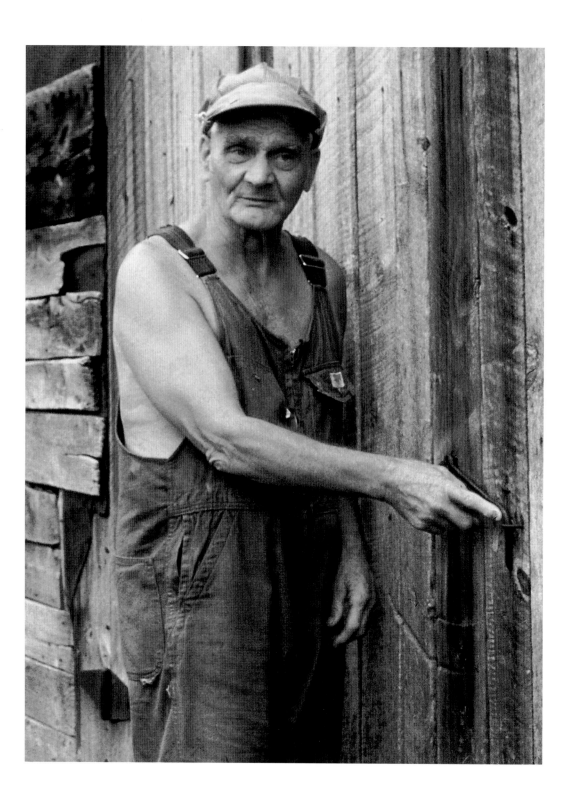

Dorothy Burnham described it. Something that looked memorable on a bed, even when there was nobody under it to keep warm. A traditional, handmade piece of folk art that was also useful.

Similarly, does that copper rooster weather vane on the church have to be so realistic, so splendid? Wouldn't a wooden shingle point into the wind just as well? Be just as useful? This is where our discussion of folk art should properly unfold.

We have another set of three terms to examine: the three major categories of folk art, which also define themselves as periods in the development of folk art. There's useful folk art, there's folk art that celebrates the past, and there's personal folk art. All are found in both the house and the garden. Again, let's look at them one at a time.

Useful Folk Art

From those pre-Confederation days right into the middle of this century a folk art object had several ways to qualify as folk art. Much folk art was anonymous—that is, we no longer (or never did) know the name of the maker. This was a carry-over from the collections of anonymous oral folklore. For folk art, it was usually enough to know that a piece fit the tradition. It was decorative, and if it was not actually beautiful, its maker had clearly tried to raise it one level past the commonplace. Next, the piece was probably useful in addition to being aesthetically pleasing: a superbly carved letter box, for example, could be folk art. A sampler that taught the alphabet, numbers and stitchery is pretty and useful, definitely folk art. A carved maple-sugar

Facing page: George Cockayne had a flexible imagination. He was able to see people, animals and strange creatures hidden in pieces of wood even before he began carving them. (Erica Claus)

mould, or a painted wardrobe or clothing chest (there were no closets, by the way, in those early Canadian houses)—all useful and unquestionably folk art.

There are those early portraits of moon-faced kids with huge heads and flat features; those families with a dog standing stiffly outside the cabin. Many of these were painted by itinerant artists, who painted the bodies in the winter when they were unable to travel and then painted in the faces and other details after arriving at the customer's house in the warmer months. Useful? Yes. That portrait went along with the ancestral Bible flyleaf in importance as a visual record of the family. And they told us how people dressed in Canada's early days; how they lived, what they played with, what they ate and so on. For folklorists, this was the point. Besides, there's little advantage in arguing that a painting is not art or at least meant as art!

In his documentation of folk art, Marius Barbeau, arguably Canada's best and certainly one of our earliest folklorists, consistently adhered to these principles of usefulness and anonymity, with certain very interesting exceptions. Barbeau and his colleagues explored the French Canadian oral tradition more deeply than anyone before him had done. He recorded songs, fiddle tunes, stories, folk speech; you name it, he wrote it down in his upside-down and backwards, da Vinci–style script in countless journals. He recorded widely on wax cylinders, wire and tape, and published amazing numbers of papers and books. He connected French Canada with Renaissance France in many intriguing ways, though this is an area beyond our discussion. Barbeau also assembled a wealth of three-dimensional objects, the backbone of the early folk art collection at the Geological Survey of

Facing page: George Cockayne, a lifelong bachelor, fashioned this woman out of a cedar fence post and put her to work as a doorstop for his large workshop door. "It's nice to have a woman to come home to," he said dryly. Madoc, Ontario. (Harry Foster; CMC 75-1057)

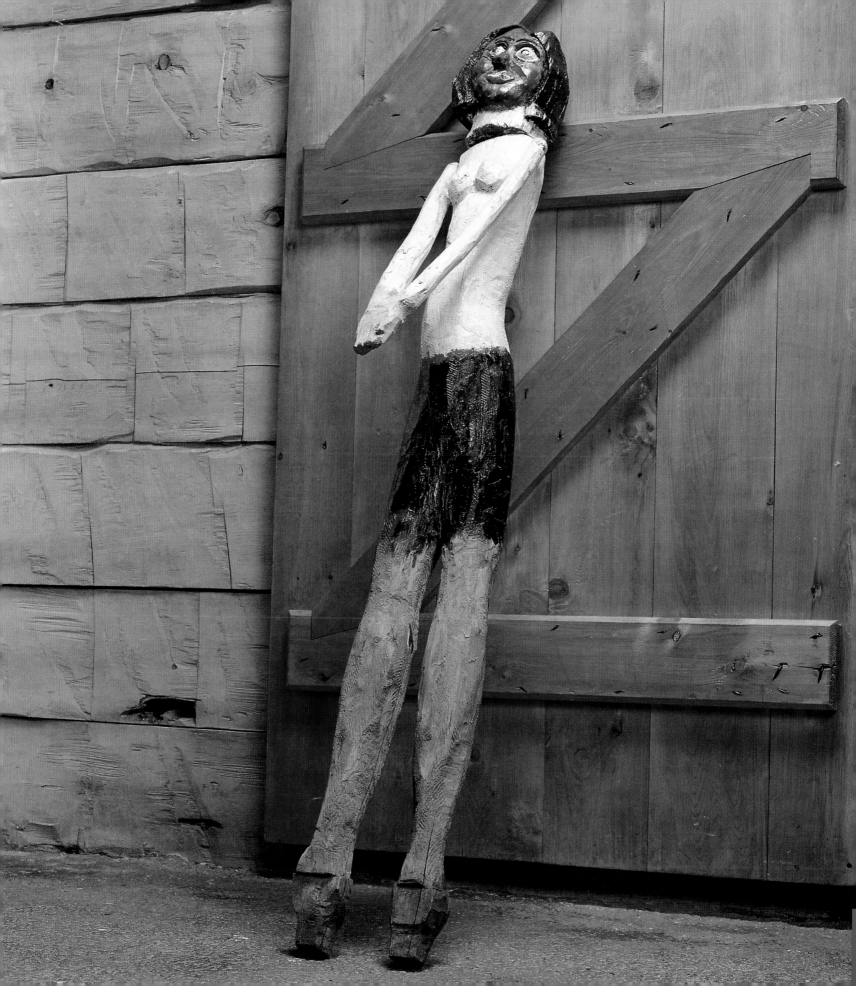

Canada and later at the National Museum of Man in Ottawa. Much of it was traditional, anonymous and decorated past the stage of pure utility.

However, he also discovered folk carvers, and for the first time did not allow them all to remain anonymous. Barbeau said of some of them, their work is traditional. They are folk. What they are producing is folk art. They must be researched and collected, even if we do break the chain of anonymity that has been so precious to purist folklorists.

This was a significant departure. Here were named folk artists, producing not the anonymous artifacts that folklorists had always sought out, but signed pieces. In a very important respect, Barbeau was looking towards the folk art movement—both creation and collection—that was to come after the midpoint of the twentieth century, and which will be discussed later in this chapter.

In short, up until about the 1920s, scholars of folklore had confined their artifact studies to anonymous, useful objects that had traditional decorations and fell clearly into the realm of folk art. By naming an artist—and yet still labelling him or her a folk artist—Barbeau was departing radically from established academic tradition and crossing a frontier in Canadian folklore studies.

Barbeau's legacy is wonderfully debatable, but the fact remains that his work will always stand at the forefront of that first generation of Canadian folk art study. Most of what he collected is indeed anonymous; much of it is useful; yet all of it is pleasing to a sometimes indefinable aesthetic sense that places it in the realm of folk art. Is it a bit too much to place Barbeau as the discoverer of folk art in Canada? Perhaps, but he certainly belongs in the first wave of its explorers.

Folk Art That Celebrates the Past

When the first folklorists set pen to paper, it was clear that their most common and oft repeated refrain was to decry the imminent loss of folk traditions, a scholarly custom that continues to the present day. The informants will die before the proper interviews can be made; the traditions will change before the old ones can be notated; and there will never be enough time (money, students, archives, etc.) for sufficient collection, documentation or interpretation.

The fact is, culture is in constant flux, and any study we are able to make is merely a snapshot of a short, and certainly finite, period. All we can do is look back at what has been done and thank our predecessors for the work they did so we can interpret that snapshot at a later date.

In Canada, official, large-scale collection of folkloric artifacts did not get under way until about 1970. Prior to that, various Canadian institutions busied themselves primarily with archaeological items and aboriginal and historical artifacts, all in addition to objects of interest to natural scientists. Indeed, before 1970, Marius Barbeau and several of his French Canadian colleagues were almost the only ones interested in folk objects at all. Folk art was, of course, always being created, but only limited attention was paid to it.

In 1970, the National Museum of Man in Ottawa (later the Canadian Museum of Civilization) began serious collection of folk objects from a variety of Canadian ethnocultural groups. A new interest in what was then called "multiculturalism" helped spur this movement, and the resulting influx of money and the hiring of a new generation of budding scholars certainly helped.

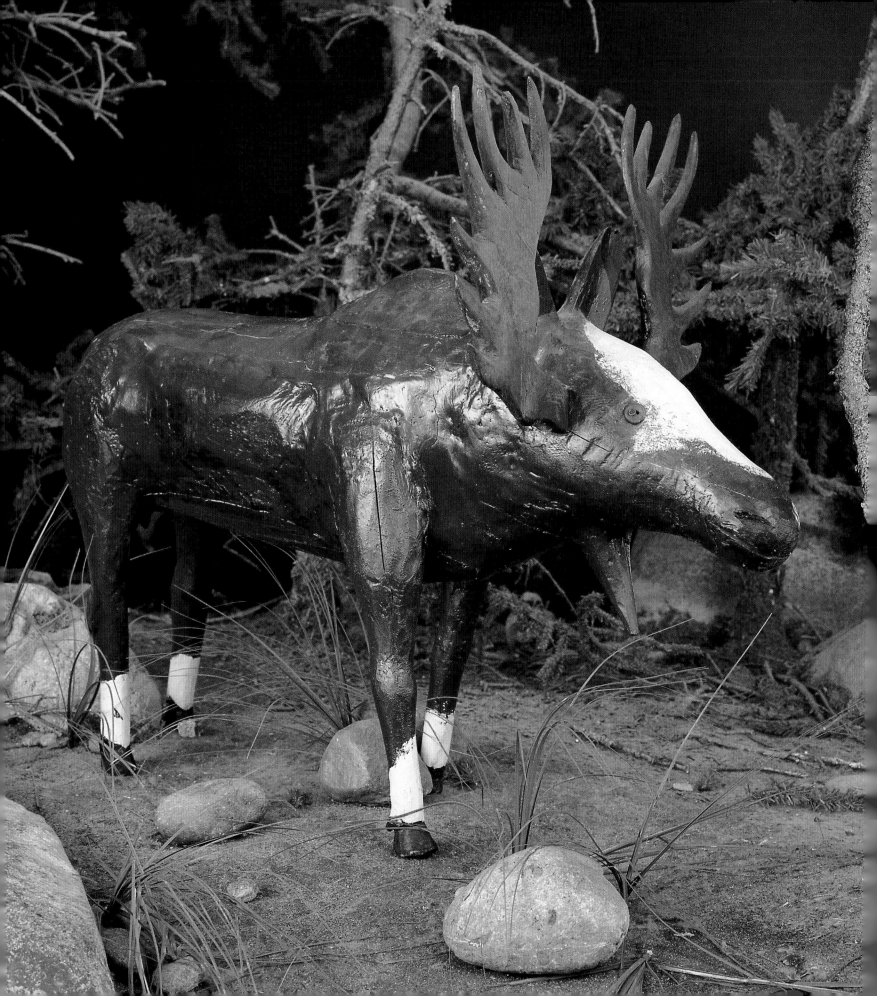

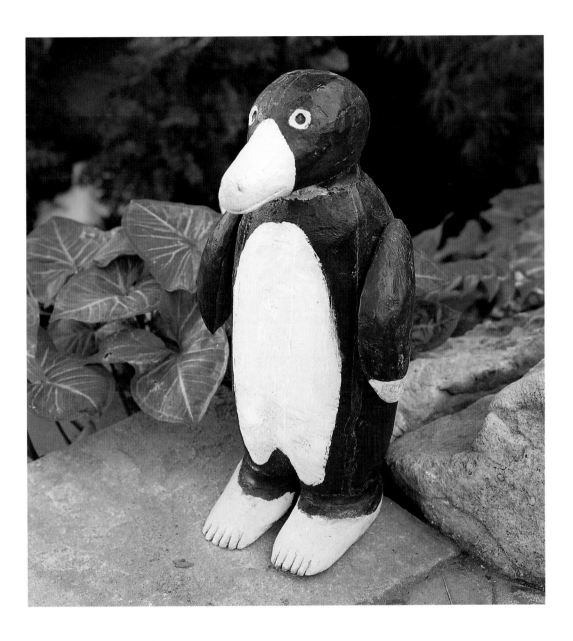

A formal penguin attributed to Alcide St. Germain of Saint-Antoine-Abbé, Quebec, who was well known for his carvings of exotic animals, including giraffes and tigers. The penguin's six-toed feet and French cuffs are wonderfully appealing. (Harry Foster; CMC 75-1034)

Facing page: This rather delicate, knee-high moose was one of a series of creatures made by Alcide St. Germain. He was particularly proud of his first moose carving, which weighed slightly more than 600 kilograms. (Harry Foster; CMC 74-813)

At approximately the same time, art and antique dealers as well as selected galleries across the country became interested in folk art because, as never before, a market had developed for these objects. Academics such as J. Russell Harper who had already been on the folk art bandwagon were suddenly justified in the marketplace in their enthusiasm for folk objects and folk art. Serious attention was paid to the whole of folk creation across Canada, including, for almost the first time, that of ethnic groups other than English or French.

Many of the first objects bought, sold and collected were of the "useful" variety mentioned above. Tobacco cutters, sugar moulds and furniture were much sought after. Words like "naïve," "vernacular" and "grass roots" began tripping off tongues in Canada's commercial, academic and museum centres. Soon, pieces of folk art that fit these descriptive words were being identified, acquired and, indeed, made by a whole new crop of artists.

Retired farmers, craftsmen and artisans of innumerable backgrounds began

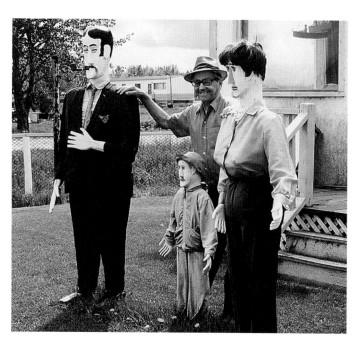

the trend of describing their former professions in miniatures. Lines of carved horses in full harness began appearing on gallery plinths. Tiny smithies appeared courtesy of local historical societies. Sleighs, ploughmen, boat models and logging scenes found their way into museums and onto collectors' mantelpieces. The folk history of the nation began to see the light of day in miniature artifact form. Folk art was suddenly credible.

Folk painters, always the poor cousins to the fine artists of whom we are justifiably proud, suddenly found their works avidly sought after by collectors. Russell Harper's remarkable exhibition at the National Gallery of Canada in 1973, called *A People's Art,* and his later books captured the Canadian imagination. We have untrained, unacademic, working-class art! And it is all ours!

Much of the folk material bought, traded and indeed created in this period was related to the feeling of celebration of our nation's past. We had Prairie painters (some famous like William Kurelek; some to become famous like Jeanne Thomarat or Ann Harbuz) depicting the brutal winters and fruitful summers of our plains. We saw the emergence of Maritime painters, such as Joe Norris and Joe Sleep from Nova Scotia, or Arch Williams of Newfoundland, recording disappearing fishing techniques, shipwrecks and lighthouses. In their own coastal way, they too were telling us who we were.

During the same era, Canada also began to understand its ethnic roots, those other than Aboriginal, English or French. Ukrainian designs became commonplace—Hutsulian Easter eggs were no longer mysterious. Ken Peacock moved from recording Newfoundland music to documenting Lithuanian customs, including highly decorated textiles. We celebrated Polish, Chinese and Icelandic folk arts—all with a Canadian veneer. And because many of those ethnic arts came from the old countries with the immigrants, we again, through these folk arts, celebrated the past. The second period of folk art creation and folk art collection was under way.

In the garden, birdhouses were suddenly discovered. These architectural miniatures often showed us models of our fantasies, a home we had actually

Facing page: Charles Gagnon with a family of his folk art lawn figures. The hand-carved wooden bodies are dressed in the fashions of Joussard, Alberta, in 1979. (Wes Mattie)

owned or wanted to build, or what we revered in our home-grown design traditions. Weather vanes changed almost overnight from wind monitors into soaring folk art, and many farmers looked up one morning to find their century-old weather vane had been "disappeared" overnight.

Whirligigs, a bit of a giggle on the back-yard fence, found serious collectors. The *patenteux* yard decorators in French Canada, long regarded as the eccentric cousins of more "serious" folk artists, came into their own in the mid '70s. *Les patenteux du Québec*—a picture book by a trio of art students— was the book every folklore scholar wished he or she had written first. Personal, whimsical (perhaps even nontraditional!) garden art had suddenly achieved recognition and legitimacy.

Personal Folk Art and the Rise of Named Folk Artists

In the previous section, I noted several Canadian folk artists by name. In the study of folk art, this naming of artists was a new development and the logical consequence of Barbeau's work in the years from 1920 to 1960. Prior to this, folklore had generally been anonymous: the teller of tales, the maker of the quilt, the designer and builder of the birdhouse were not important. It was the product, the object and its traditional roots that were critical.

But as the 1960s and 1970s wore on, named Canadian folk artists became increasingly important. A cynic would say that the forces of the marketplace insisted on identifying artists to encourage better sales. The cynic would be partly right. However, there were other reasons, such as the desire of museum

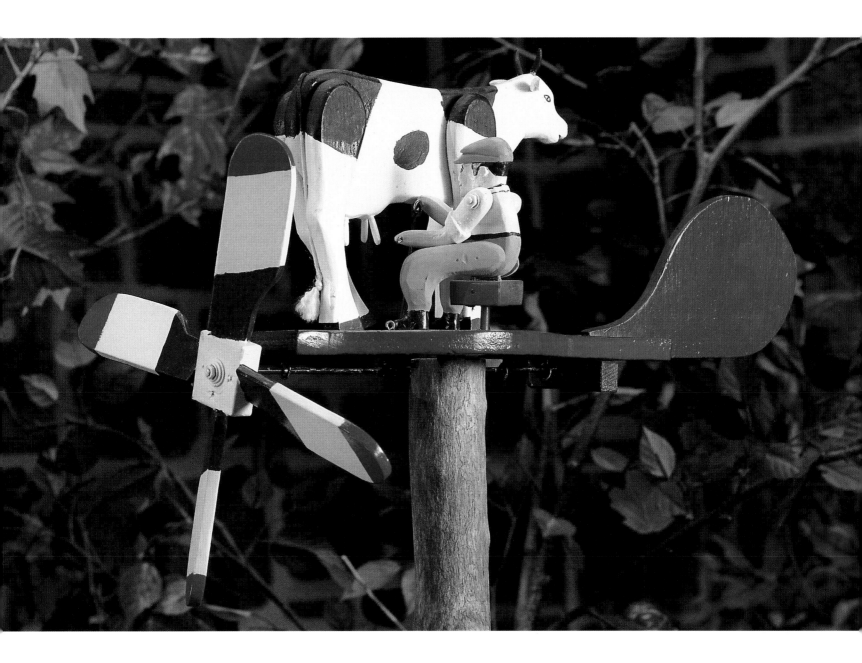

A former schoolteacher, Arthur MacNeill of St. Peter's, Prince Edward Island, created many beautifully finished whirligigs. They are incredibly detailed—note the cow's tail of braided rope—and are made with humour, showing exaggerated movement with every increase in wind speed. (Harry Foster; CMC 82-51)

professionals to establish *provenance* for objects. Where did it come from? Who did it? Where did she learn it? What was the background? Why now? Why this way? Were there other artists who influenced her? Where did they live and what did they make?

In many cases, these questions were neither asked nor answered, so brisk was the commerce; thus some information inevitably was lost. Indeed, this is the case with much of the art in the outdoor or garden category. A great deal was simply bought, traded and sold with nothing more than what the museum professionals call "tombstone" information: description, height, weight, material, colour, probable date of manufacture. The pieces had to speak for themselves. Folk art? Obviously. Provenance? Sketchy.

However, Canadian folk artists did continue to become less and less anonymous, and with this growing fame their works became less and less strictly traditional. For almost the first time, folk artists could be truly, freely artistic, carving, painting or fashioning pieces well beyond the confines of tradition. Edmond Châtigny could carve a green and pink bird with two dozen baby birds attached. George Cockayne could create what he called "bugs," four-legged creatures with big blue tongues. Clem Hibbard could decorate his yard with *Star Trek* styrofoam heads with electric blue and yellow stripes. Imagination and fantasy—indeed, released creativity—had become normal and welcome.

From the perspective of a museum or a collector, then, named folk artists—even those outside the "normal" tradition—was a not entirely undesirable development. Along with a name came the possibility of more information.

From an art-dealer and marketplace point of view, a name was essential to good sales. "This carved chicken," for example, "is a Collins Eisenhauer!" would be a good sales phrase. (The quirky and incredibly talented Eisenhauer was the Maritimes' best-known folk carver for more than a decade.) "This naked woman feeding a skunk," for an outdoor Eisenhauer example, "is destined to become a classic." And indeed it did.

On the down side, however, was a perfectly normal dealer desire to keep the whereabouts of their best-selling artists secret for as long as they could in order to become the sole "agent" of a folk artist's work. As a result, background information was frequently lost, mislaid, never known or never adequately researched.

Into this breach stepped a remarkable variety of collectors, dealers, scholars and curators who did their level best to remedy a situation that was almost out of control. Another remarkable exhibition, *The Folk Art of Nova Scotia* (1976), gave unprecedented legitimacy to contemporary folk art and also to celebrating individual folk artists. Bernard Riordan, still the director of the Art Gallery of Nova Scotia, was one of the few to see the future of folk art display, sales and study. He put together a team that selected objects, recorded biographies and wrote descriptions of a wide variety of "personal" art. Other collectors, writers and dealers followed suit, such as Bruce Ferguson, Murray Stewart, Chris and Mary Huntington, Gerald Ferguson, Blake and Ruth MacKendry, Ralph and Patricia Price, Howard Pain, Philip Shackleton and many, many others.

The National Museum of Man leapt into this foray with enthusiasm. At first, individual curators collected a spotty cluster of folk art objects. Bob

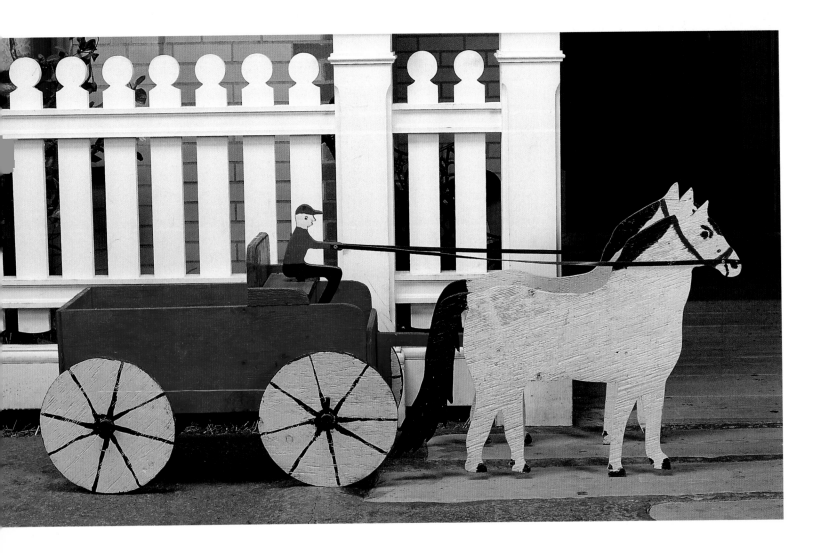

When he retired from the Corps of Commissionaires, Earl Crawford of Carleton Place, Ontario, sought to record some memories of his rural life. This horse and farm wagon model may have been a planter for the front lawn. (Harry Foster; CMC 73-538)

Facing page: Collins Eisenhauer was arguably Nova Scotia's best-known folk artist and certainly the one with the wickedest sense of humour. Pierre Trudeau and Robert Stanfield were carved for a parade float. They were seated across from one another at a card table, flanked by figures of Gerald Regan, then premier of Nova Scotia, and David Lewis, the leader of the NDP. It took the artist a full year to carve all four figures. After the parade, they all became lawn ornaments. (Harry Foster; CMC 75-914, 75-919)

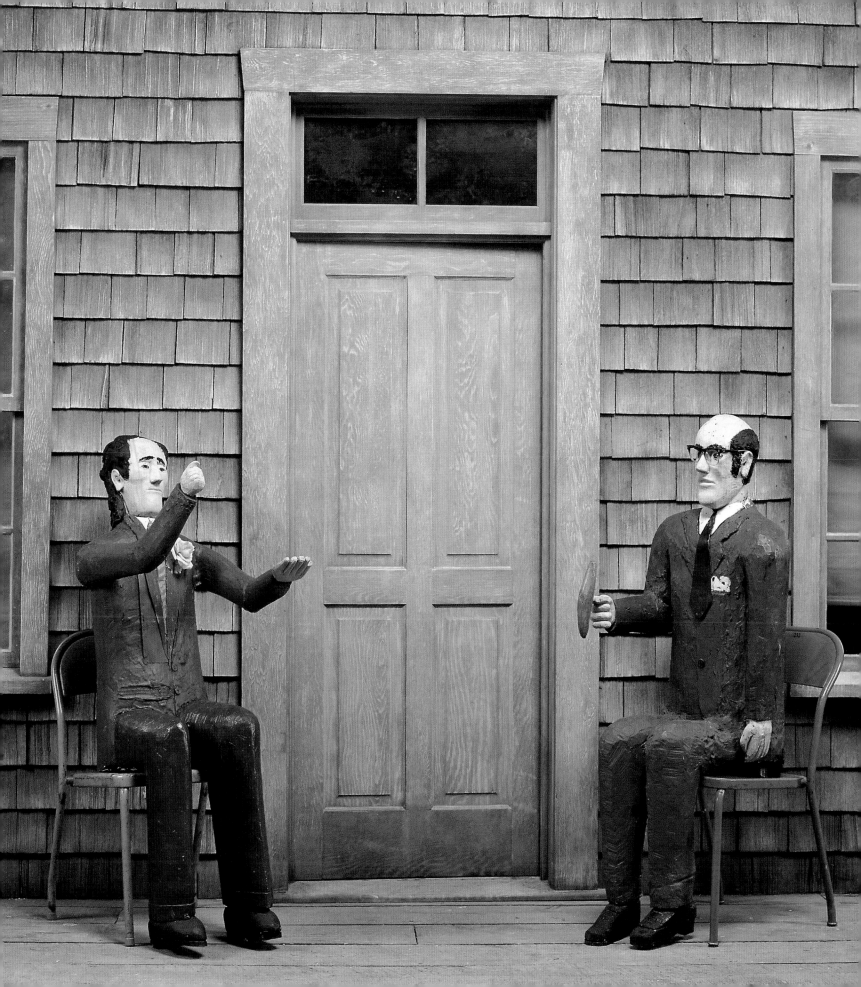

Klymasz collected ethnic, primarily Slavic, objects. Magnús Einarsson concentrated on Scandanavian, but quickly branched into "mainstream" folk art. Carmen Roy and Paul Carpentier pursued French Canadian artifacts. Gradually, other curators joined the team, and the collections grew.

At the hub of all this was Curator Wes Mattie, who plunged into folk art collection head first. He scoured the country for first-class creations, recognizing instinctively that the objects were worth preserving, and that the folk art phenomenon was temporary. He bought from the artists themselves, from galleries and dealers, from scholars, flea markets and purveyors of all sorts. What he could not justify on his budget, he photographed by the thousands *in situ*. A picture book of this work has yet to be compiled.

Most important, however, Mattie procured for the national collections the amassed materials of many other serious and prolific collectors. Although he was criticized at the time for this, these collections became the bedrock of the almost thirty thousand folklore and folk art objects in what was now called the Canadian Museum of Civilization—the most comprehensive assemblage in the nation. Mattie arranged for the acquisition of the Nettie Sharpe collection of Quebec folk art during this period, the Ralph and Patricia Price Collection and many other notable troves of named and unique pieces. It was the view of some that commerce overcame scholarship in these acquisitions, but there is no question that if the collections had not come to the museum, almost every Canadian folk art artifact would have vanished into the hands of private American collectors, never to be seen again in Canada.

Gerald Ferguson, a professor of studio art in Nova Scotia, as well as a collector and practising artist, wrote to Mattie in 1980. On the subject of buying whole collections, he said, "I regard it as a very wise and economical strategy. It's like having a variety of knowledgeable curators without having to pay salaries."

Garden and outdoor art, those delicious expressions of exuberance that many folk artists chose to keep and display for themselves, was an undercurrent through all three of these periods of folk art study, collection and analysis. Barbeau acquired trade signs and other outdoor carvings as they came to his attention. Useful, you'll remember, but aesthetic.

The celebration of the past found its way into birdhouse designs; whirligigs spoke eloquently about sawyers, millers, milkers and sailors; and weather vanes celebrated oxen, horse-drawn vehicles of a past age, as well as roosters and fish, some of each with religious overtones.

Finally, individual and undeniably quirky folk artists decorated their personal Edens with steel women, well-known politicians, and yes, lions and tigers and bears. We shall look at Canadian folk art outdoors more thoroughly in the next section.

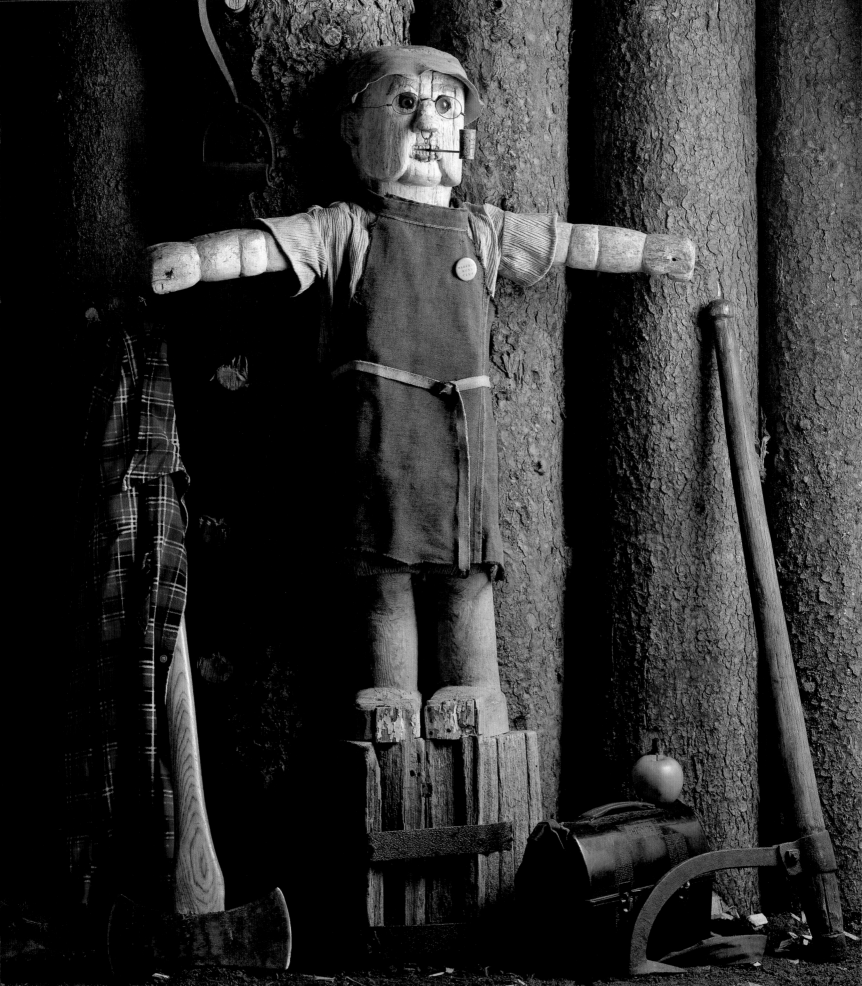

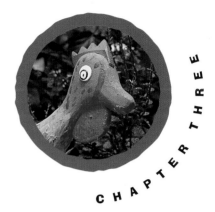

CHAPTER THREE

Canadian Folk Art Outdoors

WE SPEAK OF "man's home being his castle," but in fact it is the land surrounding the home—that is, the garden—where one can leave a truly individual stamp. It is there that a person's individuality can best and most readily be expressed. This area is truly the expression of a personal Eden, quite literally a paradise outside the cave. The cave has no real importance except to keep out the rain.

Houses are only rarely built by the owner, but the garden is always conceived, planned, revamped and finally decorated by the owner. He

"Clem" represents process. Beneath all his accessories, he is a working scarecrow: his carved arms are able to remain outstretched in classic scarecrow posture. Just as an antique house has rooms, ells, chimneys and dormers added by different generations, so Clem has gradually acquired glasses, a nose ring, clothes and a lapel pin. (Harry Foster; CMC 77-287)

or she chooses where and whether there will be trees, flowers or vegetables; and decides whether there will be services for birds (water, food, housing, a swimming area), insects (bees, butterflies, etc.) or other creatures.

More important, the owner decides whether to display outdoor artistic expressions of any sort, ranging from a weather vane on a roof to decorations hung in trees at eye level, to moving or stationary three-dimensional objects at ground level. It is in the yard that imaginative juices can truly flow, where outdoor self-expression can flourish and be displayed not only to the owner and his housemates but also to the wider audience of neighbours and passers-by. This is the two-fold excitement and importance of yard art: it is creativity at the level of pure self-satisfaction, and it is also movement towards an artistic performance for those outside the family unit.

There are two concepts at work here. First, everyone has a creative impulse, whether fleeting or lasting. It is a human universal, expressed orally ("Some people can just *tell* jokes"); personally ("Some people just *know* how to dress"); or artistically ("She's so *clever* with her hands"). Some, of course, may not choose to express their creative impulses, but they have them nevertheless and recognize them in others.

Second, everyone has access to or is acquainted with a garden or yard—in every province and region of Canada. Either a person has a garden, wishes he or she had a back-yard garden, grows plants in a sunny apartment window, or if none of the above are possible, admires other people's efforts at taming or creating that back-yard Eden. Yard art, three-dimensional objects designed to decorate these personal (and possibly "public") spaces, merely marries these two concepts: physical expressions of creativity displayed in a personal outdoor space.

Having thought through the reasons why we might put folk art outdoors, let's consider what sorts of objects logically end up there.

The Weather Vane Story

First, a little history, and the word "little" is used here advisedly.

The fact is, although every scholar wants to prove that his subject is remarkably ancient and therefore credible as a worthwhile pursuit, much venerable outdoor folk art has simply rotted away. As to its history, we're guessing. But these are educated guesses.

Weather and predicting the weather is important to every agrarian society. Even an ancient farmer in the Fertile Crescent had to know when to plant, when to water (or not to water) and, most important, when to harvest. Before any sophisticated weather prognostication was developed, a farmer was on his own with his folk traditions. He knew, because his father had taught him, which way the prevailing wind blew, and thus to a certain degree he knew when the weather was likely to be fair.

He also knew that when the wind changed, it was likely to bring rain. Knowing that the wind had changed was an essential skill; hence the first weather vanes. These were pretty simple gadgets at first, probably nothing more than a strip of cloth on a pole of some sort. It would always face the wind, its tail stretching out behind, but even in the lightest breeze it imparted the necessary information. Fair wind, plant now. Nor'easter coming (or equivalent cataclysm over the Euphrates), don't cut the hay.

If a farmer had a really cool red pennant, it only follows that the farmer in the next field put up one of another colour, and maybe his was shaped like a windsock. It was a little different, a personal touch. Folk art weather vanes with built-in aesthetics were born. However, in the dust of history, both banner and windsock have long since returned to the soil, so there is no artifact evidence of all this. It remains one of our educated guesses.

Some guesses are based upon stories, however. Folklorists dote on the provable tale of the first metal weather vane from ancient Greece. In Athens, during the first century B.C., a respected astronomer named Andronikos Kyrrhestes oversaw the building of an eight-sided structure called a *horologion,* which still exists today. It was a combination sundial, weather vane and water clock, and was placed just below the Parthenon for the townsfolk of Athens to use when ever necessary. This particular building was called the Tower of Winds, because on each wall, on the outside—in much the same spirit as outdoor folk art— were carved the figures of the eight principal winds with their names. On the north side, for example, is a relief carving of Boreas, the North Wind, who is dressed warmly, looks quite windblown, and is blowing into a large shell. We'll dispense with the inventory of the other wind figures, but they're all there.

On top of the building was a metal weather vane of Triton holding what seemed to be a wand. Triton, you'll remember, was the god of the sea who

Facing page: More than a century old, these heron carvings were used as decoys in the Niagara peninsula. When heron hunting was outlawed in the 1870s, these lovely characters were retired, but were reincarnated as lawn ornaments between the wars. In the late 1970s, they came to the National Museum of Man, now the Canadian Museum of Civilization, where they started their third career as specimens of outdoor folk art. (Harry Foster; CMC 78-267, 78-268)

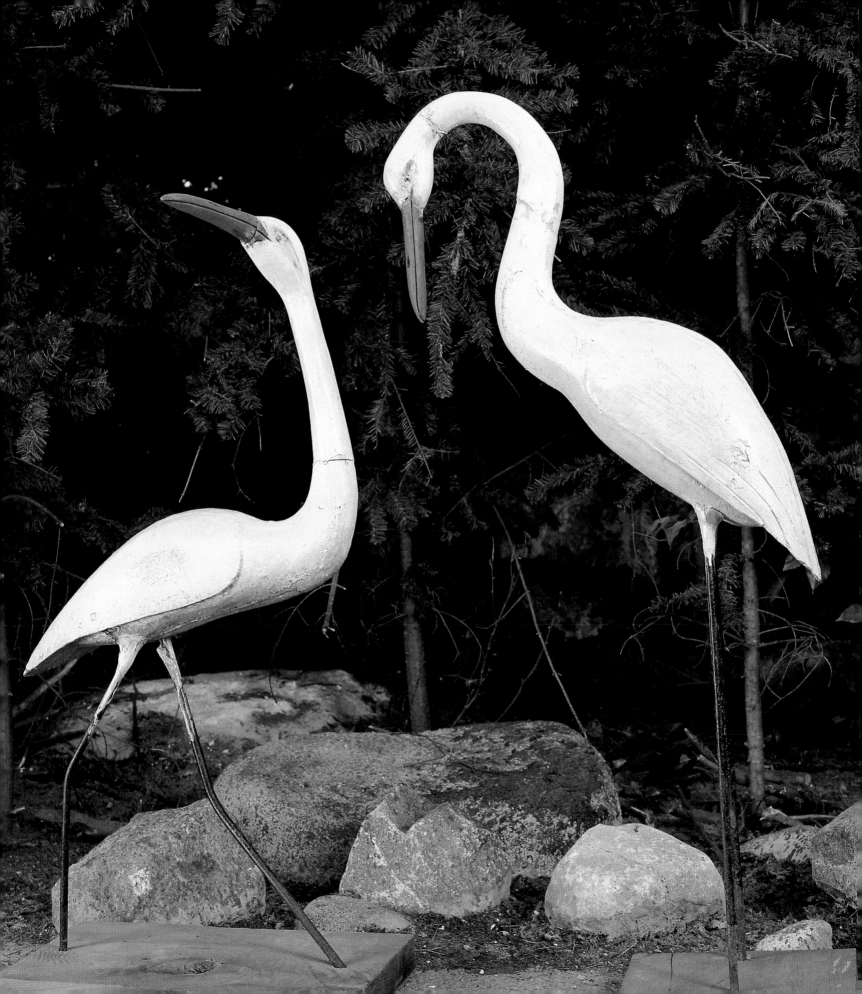

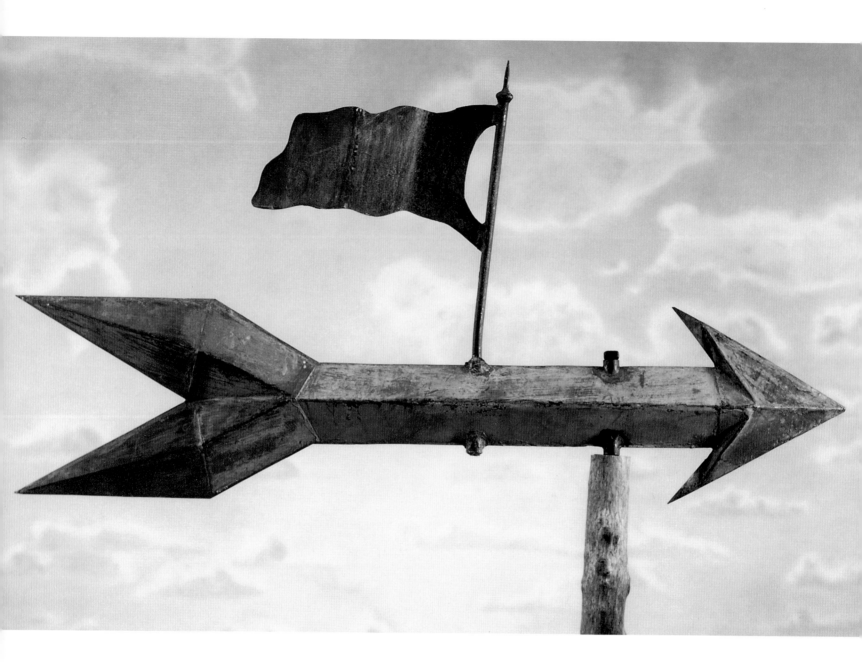

A soldered-tin arrow weather vane sports a French national flag, leaving no room for doubt as to where the sentiments of its maker lie. The banneret-style weather vane, of which this is a rather Spartan example, was a common design among vane creators. (Harry Foster; CMC 80-138)

had a male top half and what looked like a mermaid bottom half. Athens was filled with sailors, after all, and knowing wind direction wasn't just for farmers. When the wind blew, Triton swivelled and his wand pointed downwards to the appropriate wall, indicating which of the eight Winds were at work. Although, like the Fertile Crescent windsocks, Triton disappeared some time in the last twenty-one centuries, this was the first recorded, official and, we might add, artistic weather vane.

A few centuries later in Europe, farmers and sailors still had to know the wind directions for the same agricultural or sailing reasons, and weather vanes were still just as useful. Scandanavian archaeologists assert that Viking sailors used wind vanes on their longboats in roughly the ninth century, and that churches also had public and decorated weather vanes a century or two later. First function, then form.

Weather lore was learned, passed on by word of mouth and absorbed by the next generation for centuries. Rhymes helped, as did songs and anecdotes. But when those same Europeans began to flood into North America, suddenly all their precious weather wisdom was worthless. The winds blew the wrong way; the plants were different and gave different signals. None of the rhymes told the truth. Only the folk art weather vane was consistent.

There is one more story of which folklorists approve. Shortly after the Vikings began using weather vanes, one of the Popes (which one is rarely specified in this story) was captivated by the story of Christ being betrayed by Peter three times before the cock crowed. He decreed, therefore, that every

Roman Catholic house of worship have a rooster placed on its roof or steeple to remind those gazing upwards that they must do all in their power not to duplicate St. Peter's mistake.

True or not (and most now agree the story is probably not true), the cock weather vane became one of the standards in church architecture. This is especially the case in Canada, more particularly in Quebec. Barns, churches and wayside crosses all sported weather vanes in this and the last century, and a great majority were weathercocks. Again, function was essential, but decorative form was running a close second. Folk art was on the rooftops.

The weather vane story is a long one, but it indicates how art in the garden evolved from a purely utilitarian object to the next level of pure decoration.

A Shorter Story about Whirligigs

Despite the Tigris and Euphrates Rivers, Syria has historically been a dry area, where there were few central water supplies. Water for farming had to be moved to where the crops could logically be grown, so pumps were devised very early on that were able simply to lift the water into irrigation ditches. Some of these pumps were people powered, others were beast powered, oxen or donkeys being the animals of choice. Still other specialty pumps that used the wind were designed by brilliant Arabic engineers. Early versions of these pumps looked remarkably like the paddle wheels on Mississippi river boats. Set into the ground, the wind would catch the top of the paddle wheel and swish the water up and over from a main water source into a smaller ditch for the crops.

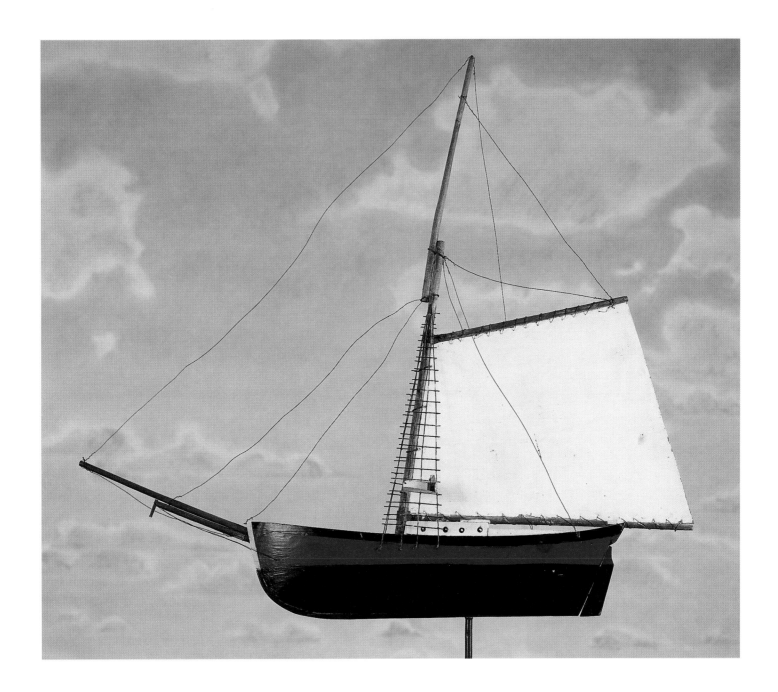

It should come as no surprise that geography can influence the choice
of subject matter for folk artists. This sailing sloop weather vane
was found in La Have, Nova Scotia, where fish weather vanes were also
very common. In the interior provinces, such as Quebec and Ontario,
roosters, cows, horses and other farm animals tend to predominate as
themes. (Harry Foster; CMC 77-278)

All three pump systems used cogs and gears and principles of motion that everyone recognized, observed and eventually understood. And in the last instance, the wind was used to make the cogs and gears work. Exactly the same principles drive the whirligig.

Later European windmill mechanics gave yet another technological push to the whirligigs. The sails of a windmill, whether from Greece or Holland, mimic a child's pinwheel as well as many types of traditional whirligig. Even later in history, miniature or model windmills in front of the house were yet another logical development, so logical that you can see miniature working windmills this very day on lawns from Newfoundland to British Columbia. Other than on the Prairies, windmills have not been a particularly well-known Canadian technology. Windmills on the front lawn are miniaturized folk art on the move.

The point is that a working, "useful" technology could easily have spilled over into the decorative, and in this case, outdoor folk arts. Just as folk art weather vanes developed from a crucial tool, so too could whirligigs have developed from an observed and miniaturized technology. Again, just an educated guess.

One more idea: early Canadian houses had cooking fires in large stone or brick fireplaces, where all meal preparation had to be done. One of the triumphs of meat cookery was known as a "spit jack." This was an advanced, eighteenth-century clockwork rotisserie that hung from the top of the fireplace damper and had a lower hook that suspended the meat over the fire. One hung a plucked chicken, a haunch or roast on the lower hook, and the clockwork in the spit jack would turn the meat back and forth slowly over the flames, ticking like a large, slow clock. The first spit jack I ever saw, at Upper Canada Village in Morrisburg, Ontario, with its clicking gears and turning motion, reminded me strongly of a whirligig mechanism. It is possible I was thinking of Ralph Boutillier's Nova Scotia whirli-birds, which though wind- rather than clockwork-powered, also have the same clicking gear mechanisms trapped inside their metal feathers to make their wings flap. Again, this is merely an educated guess.

Other Outdoor Folk Art

One of the main problems of those ancient farmers raising crops in the Fertile Crescent was pests. Birds to be more specific. Birds will eat everything that grows, and that fact has changed little from then till now. How to chase those birds away? Scarecrows are the solution.

Early scarecrows were probably made from live (or dead) crows. Tie a crow by one foot to a pole on a length of cord and his flapping and distress will certainly keep the others at bay. Or hang him dead from another pole: same effect. Or put a model of a crow's enemy, such as an owl you carved during the winter, on a pole in the middle of a field. I sense the beginning of folk art! (Some say the owls are lures to bring in more crows for destruction by the farmer; but whatever the actual use, the eureka folk-art-carving moment remains.)

There are two ways of explaining folk art here. First, the "person" scarecrow is an age-old piece of folk art, known almost everywhere crops are grown. Dress him, accessorize him, be sure to add a hat, and you have a genuine, traditional folk art piece. It's no accident that museum collections

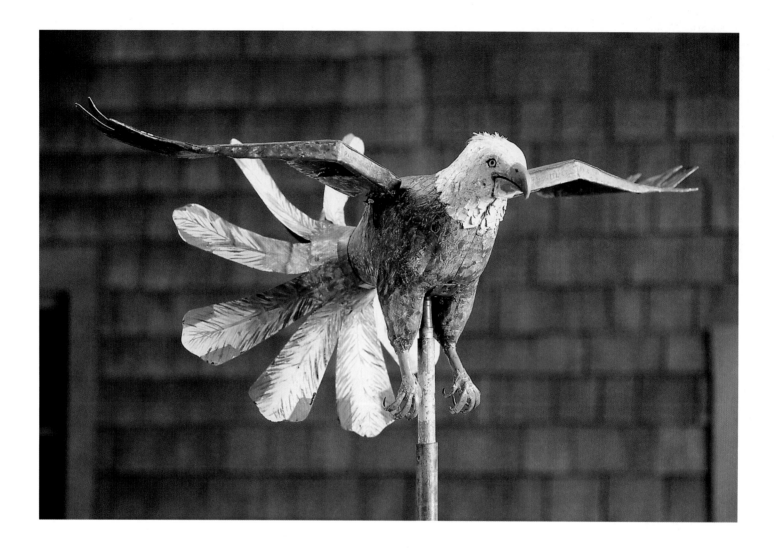

Already a dab hand at painting and model-ship building, in the 1970s Ralph Boutillier of Milton, Nova Scotia, turned his considerable mechanical skills to making really impressive whirligigs with sophisticated gear-driven inner workings. As the tail feathers turn in the wind, the eagle's wings flap slowly. (Harry Foster; CMC 76-474)

Facing page: Kost Pawlyk settled in Elk Point, Alberta, and made monumental birdhouse trees. A metal trunk and branches were hung with dozens of painted birdhouses. At the top of the tree he placed one of these splendid birds with double, sometimes triple, wings. Mr. Pawlyk painted the bird whirligigs in traditional Hutsulian designs, making them look as if they had just flown through a Ukrainian Easter egg. (Harry Foster; CMC 81-236)

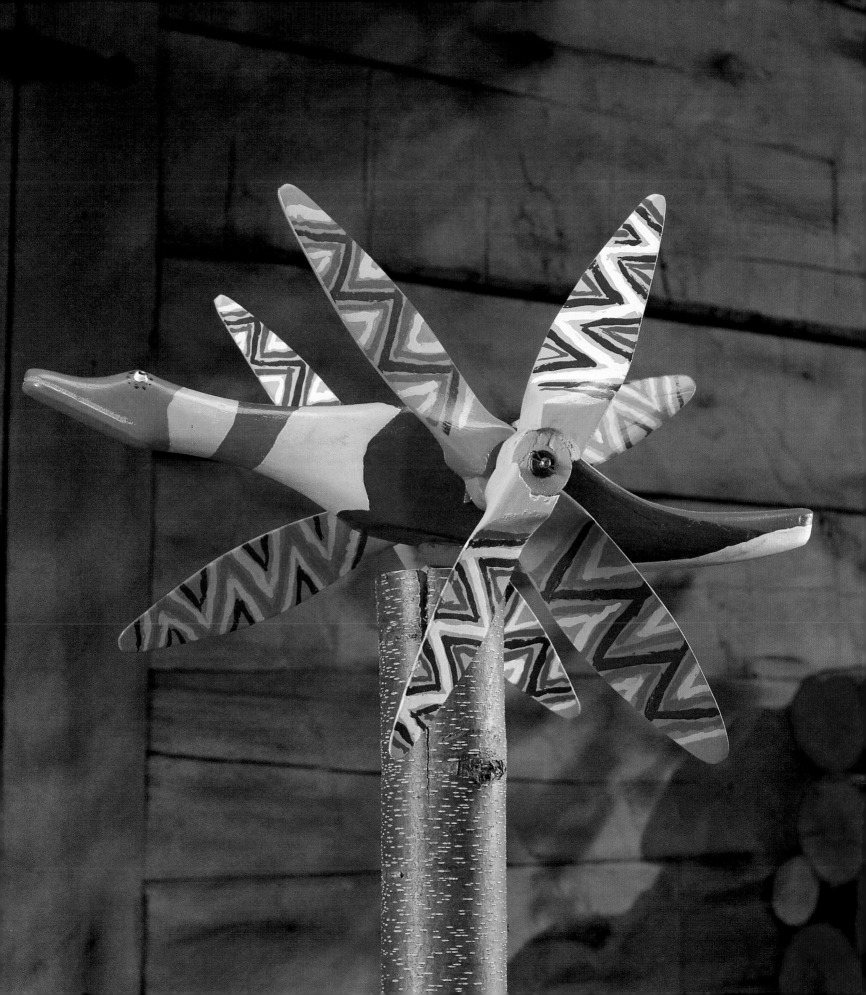

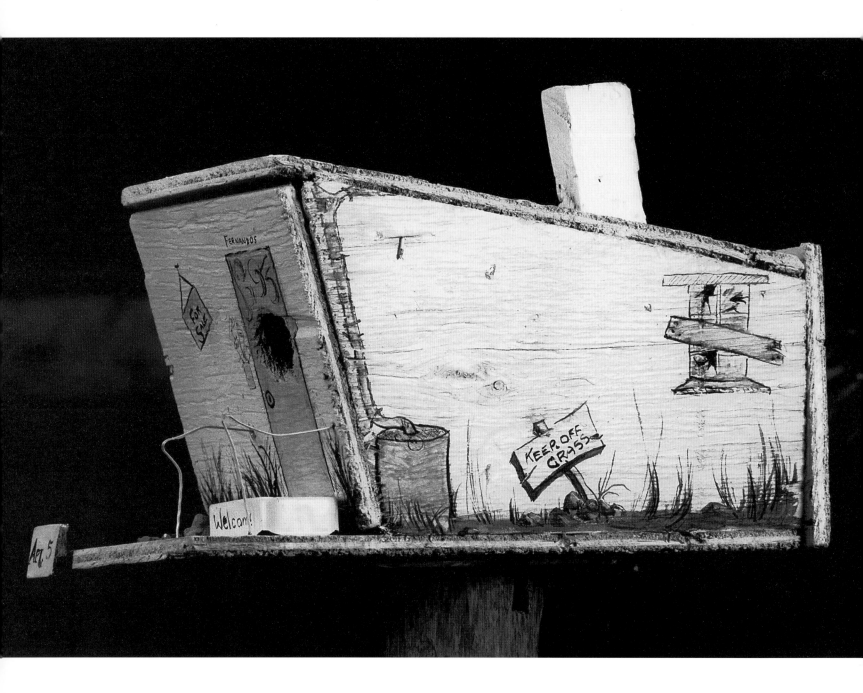

Made by schoolboys in Norway House, Manitoba, in the 1960s, this birdhouse has it all. A sardine-can stoop is flanked by hairpin bannisters. There is even a glued-on rock garden in addition to paintings on every wall. The "Fernando's," over the door is possibly a misinterpretation of "Hernando's Hideaway," a popular song written for the Broadway musical *Pajama Game.* (Harry Foster; CMC 70-203)

boast plenty of scarecrows. He's one of the characters Avon Neal and Ann
Parker examine in their landmark book, *Ephemeral Folk Figures.* The other
ephemera they touch on are harvest figures and snowmen, and these will
be discussed below. The fact to remember about ephemeral figures, however,
is that they rarely last. A scarecrow is not something one is likely to put
in a closet for the winter and bring out again for next season. And seldom
is a snowman a keeper.

Second, the folk art collection at the Canadian Museum of Civilization
has a great many bird figures. Some are clearly "scarecrows"; the owls in
particular. Others, such as eagles with huge spread wings, might also qualify
in this category. Still others are models of shore birds, chickens, turkeys
made from big fans of tree fungus and so on. All are folk art, and some were
useful, while some are meant purely as outdoor decorations.

Other useful folk art birds include decoys. Decoys were originally made
as working birds, to draw the ducks and geese and herons down out of
the skies so hunters could take them home or to market. In parts of Canada,
herons were considered a sporting bird until well into the 1920s, and the
national collections contain several heron decoys. When heron hunting
was outlawed, those same decoys became lawn ornaments. Clearly carved by
folk artists of some considerable talent, they found a new life centre stage
between the house and the road.

There is an astonishing variety of other working decoys: huge geese waddle,
cork ducks float; some floating ducks even have keels to keep them headed
into the wind as real ducks would be. Some working ducks have wires, hooks

and eyes and other hardware so their "sets" would not become separated. Hunting camps often had duck boats with a "set" of decoys for each boat.

Some decoys are "stick ups," sporting a single leg the hunter could plunge into the sand. My personal favourite is a headless goose whose neck curves into the water, giving the impression to the birds above that he is feeding contentedly.

When their working lives finished, decoys became a much sought-after folk art. A decorator's delight: portable, beautiful, desirable. At auction, carved birds by named and talented artists brought astronomical prices, only to end their days on a piano in a suburban living room. The decoys are outdoor folk art that moved from work to outdoor display and finally came indoors from the cold.

A Note about Birdhouses

Birdhouses are another major facet of outdoor folk art that we've barely covered and that certainly deserves our attention. Of all wildlife forms in North America, birds seem to come the closest to our dwellings without fear. It's no accident that birdwatching is a national sport. Think of the variety, the colour, the song, the movement of birds. A soaring hawk or a hovering hummingbird; a red-winged blackbird crowing on a cattail, or a mischievous whiskey-jack. A natural kaleidoscope for all the senses.

Our link with the birds may be—for many of us—our last real link with the wild, with raw nature without a fence between Them and Us. And there's something we can do for birds. We can *feed* them, although, interestingly,

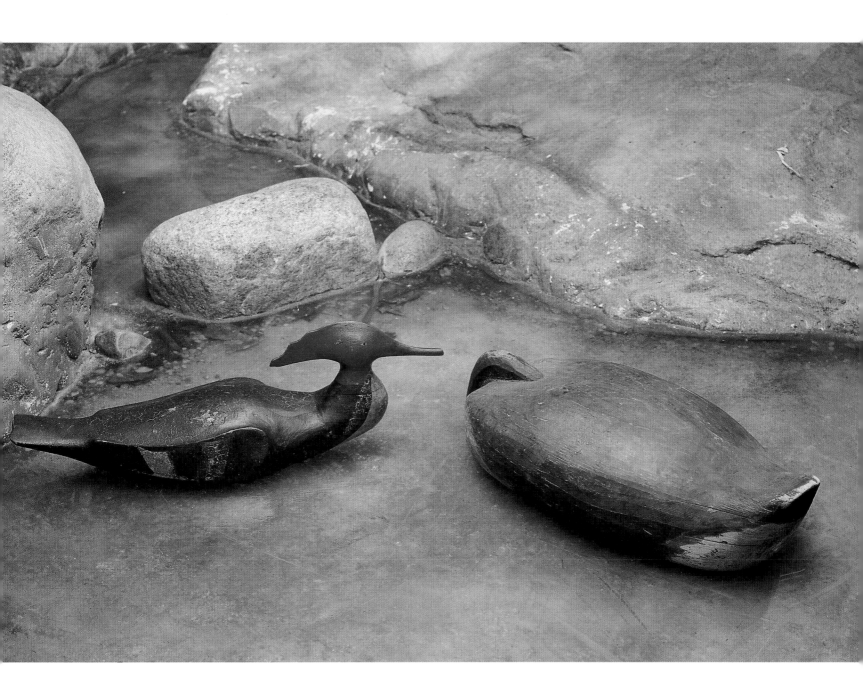

Decoy carving is a perfect opportunity for a folk artist to combine function with form. The decoy is undoubtedly useful, but as folk art, it is also undeniably beautiful. The fish-eating merganser duck, with its wonderful red crest, contrasts nicely with the feeding-goose decoy, whose neck disappears under water, making it unnecessary to carve a head. (Harry Foster; CMC 83-1417, 83-1296)

bird feeders rarely fall into the category of folk art. Or we can *house* them. It doesn't take much to make the basic, useful item: four slabs of wood, a roof and a floor, and a little hole. But at the same time, the birdhouse offers us an opportunity to do something for ourselves. Will a model of our childhood home on the back-yard fence bring some fond memories? Or tell something to our children? How about Grandpa's barn, painted up in red the way he did it? Or the church in town? (There's one of these in the national collections with a working miniature weather vane on top. Folk art on folk art.) The summer cottage? The magnificent mansion on the hill?

We can exercise our imaginations on the birdhouse, paint it with multi-coloured dots we'd never dare to use on our own house. We can remember our professions through a birdhouse: a ship, a mine, a silo or a lumber camp. And all the time we can provide a spot for nature to rest, live, breed and act as yet another layer of decoration in our back yard. Does that cardinal flitting by lift the spirit with its crimson plumage? Or his more demure mate in muted orange and brown? It's a rhetorical question. They're almost a cure for seasonal affective disorder by themselves. Outdoor folk art with a purpose.

There'll Be Some Changes Made

The exuberant explosion of outdoor folk art in Canada, like all good things, like all things in culture, eventually changed.

The Canadian folk art "furnace," the energy, vitality, inventiveness, imagination and humour, roared for almost a century, first in a quiet way, then in a burst of heat, light and sound. From the 1960s until the end of the 1980s, outdoor folk artists joyfully converted their gardens and yards into galleries of personal inspiration and display, decorating their landscapes as Canadians had never done before. It was almost un-Canadian in its intensity.

This was the era of the French Canadian *patenteux* movement, which certainly deserves special attention. In the '70s and '80s these outdoor "tinkerers" hit their stride. "Tinkerers" as a translation does not really do justice to these artists who were, quite simply, producing outdoor folk art specimens never seen before. These were not conservative walking-stick carvers or miniature makers. Their productions were frequently so bizarre that folklorists had to look long and hard before they agreed it was folk art at all.

What gave rise to the *patenteux,* I believe, was the fact that during these three fruitful decades, an entire generation of folk artists had grown up with television. They knew the world as no previous artisans had been able to do. They had seen the beasts of Africa and the penguins of Antarctica; and they reproduced these in their yards. They used found objects as never before: bizarre root figures with tiny, wildly painted heads and long ungainly limbs. Not just one or two, but dozens, some piled suggestively on others.

One Quebec artist built a concrete lion perched on a red and white fountain. Another constructed a blousy figure of a straw-hatted black woman sitting on a porch. She waved at passing motorists when a hidden string was pulled by her gleeful owner, seated in the living room. Others created veritable forests of carved birds. Still other *patenteux* mixed birdhouses, model airplanes and decorated Javex bottles, all whirling together into a jungle of movement and colour. One million bottle caps were strung into a fence and uncountable sculptures.

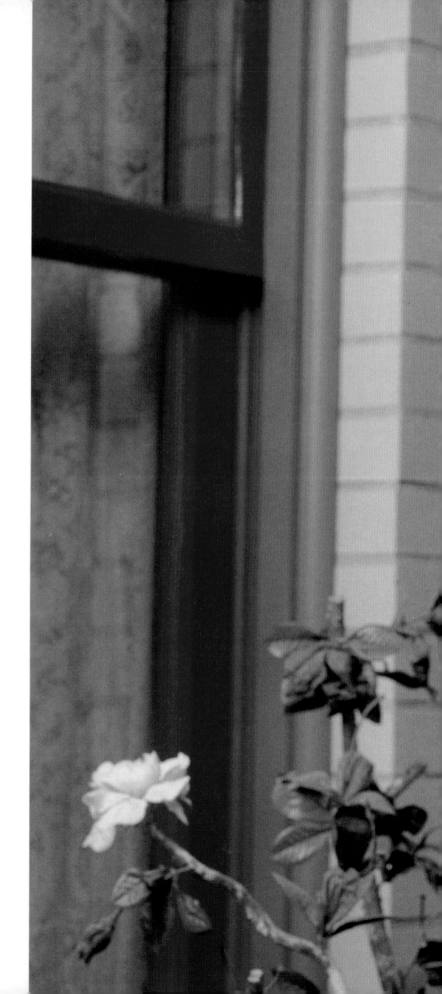

Made in Picton, Ontario, in the
mid 1970s, Elwood Sharpe's
wren house, which looks like
Red Riding Hood's birthplace,
sports a carved pine tree topped
with a bird in full flight. (Harry
Foster; CMC 90-168)

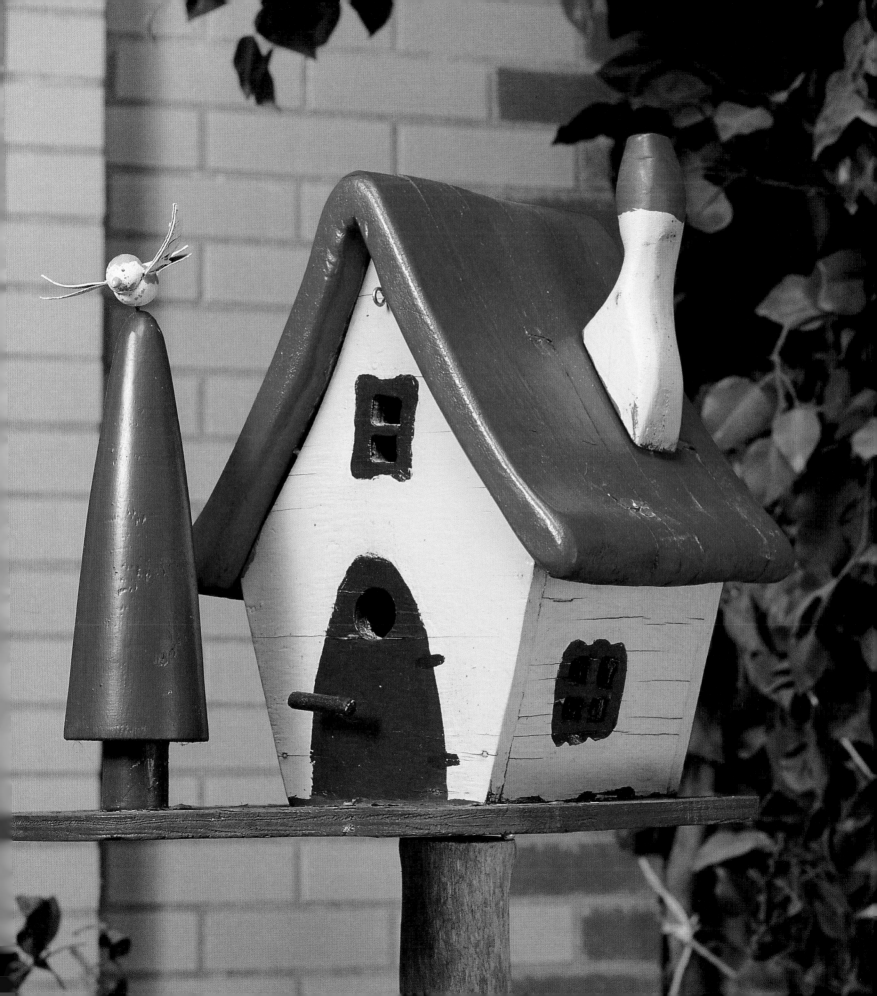

But by 1990, the production of yard art, as we have been considering it, had stopped.

Folk artists lost their ardour to create. The fervour to design something ever bigger, more colourful, more outrageous stilled. Those objects that were good enough to sell, sold. Others, like the wind cloth in the Fertile Crescent, returned from whence they had come.

Canadian gardens, however, did not become deserts, devoid of any decoration or statuary. This was not a case of disappearance, but of modification. The urge to decorate, to make one's front lawn different from that of one's neighbours, was still very much alive. What happened was the advent of faux folk art, and it happened while all the folklorists were not looking.

Dealers suddenly noticed that folk art was not being offered to galleries by pickers any more. "Grass roots" and "naïve" were words no longer being used. Now we heard "catalogue sales" and "White Rose": virtual and real stores where plasticized yard art could be bought. Rubber gnomes and fluffy Bo-Peeps appeared. Black-and-white cow silhouettes were suddenly everywhere, as were Tyvek Canada Geese, a hollow, ripstop house-wrap windsock that was mounted onto a plastic goose head and which filled realistically with every breeze. It was the same period as those plastic-coated wire-grid lawn chairs that rusted through in a single season.

Instead of a full season of folk yard art, holidays suddenly became much more significant. Hallowe'en lawn decorations surfaced in the stores shortly after Labour Day. Outdoor Christmas ornaments of the most extravagant type began appearing earlier every year. Outdoor Easter, Thanksgiving, Canada

Day and harvest decorations became available in mass commercial outlets. And Canadians bought and hung and stuck them in the lawn.

In addition, the indoor decoration phenomenon—we might call it the Martha Stewart program—spilled outdoors. Straw bonnets with flowers and long ribbons were hung on front doors as if they were seasonal wreaths. Other store-bought decorator wreaths made of autumn leaves or seashells appeared.

Finally, what I call the jigsaw sculptors, for lack of a better name, primed their tools and turned out millions of painted plywood silhouettes of fat women bending over, facing away from the road. Horrified little girls watched smirking little boys pee into the bushes under the livingroom window. Black silhouette men with red neckerchiefs leaned against garage corners. Many of these came from what the jigsaw sculptors call "the pattern books": catalogues, advertised mainly in women's magazines, that sell plans, a kit, paint and even advice on how much to charge for each item. This pattern-book trend is very similar to the postwar *Popular Mechanics* and men's magazines indoor projects of forty years earlier. Were both of these developments signs of the death of folk art?

At about the same time real folk art and statuary disappeared, a revival of gardening itself took place. Like Canadian folk art, however, Canadian gardens also have a rich design history, and both are inextricably entwined.

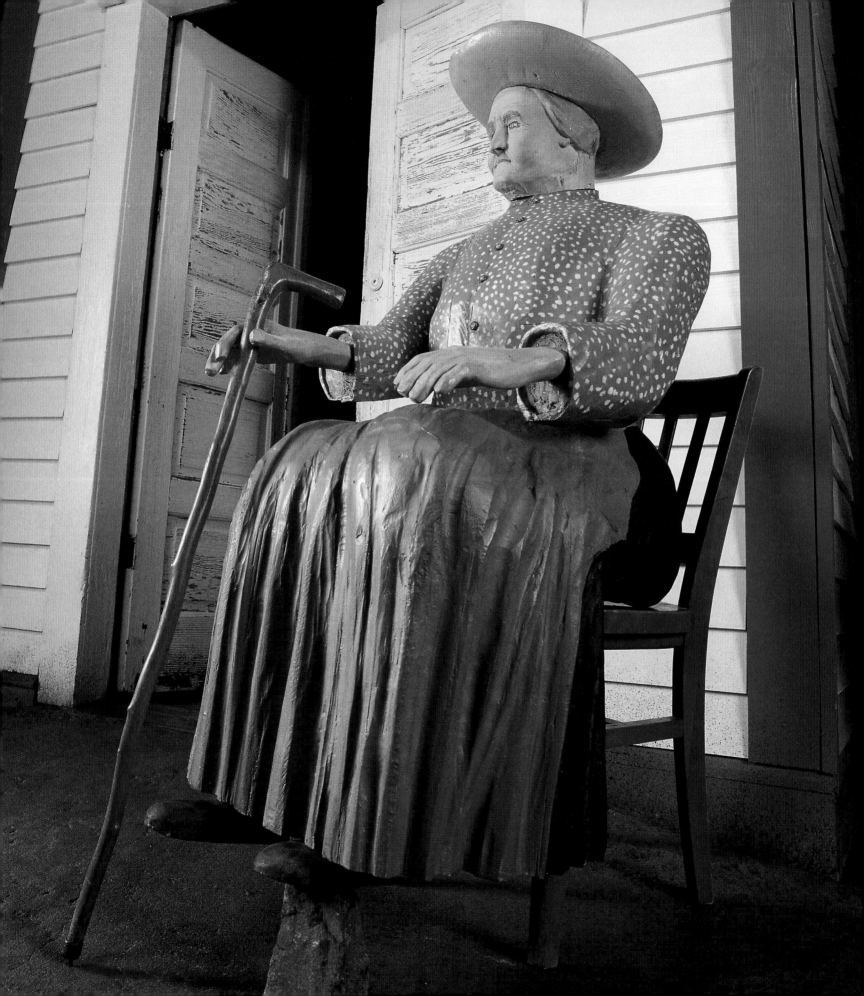

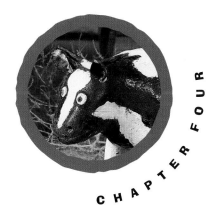

CHAPTER FOUR

From the Garden of Eden to Eden in the Garden

WITHOUT THE GARDEN in its widest sense, we would have nowhere to display outdoor folk art. Whether an artist chooses the theatrical venue of the front lawn or decides to use the more hidden and private back yard, the gardens surrounding the dwelling are his equivalent of an exhibition hall. The development of the Canadian garden has a long and fascinating history, extending to exotic and faraway places. The last thirty years have been an incredible time for gardens and for the folk art we put in them.

Representing a well-known genre of outdoor folk art, this dignified woman would have been placed on a porch to observe and be observed. Many such figures were jointed. One Quebec folk artist used to take his life-size figures for rides in the car, his passenger waving gravely to astonished drivers. (Harry Foster; CMC 78-190)

Are the Hippies to blame for our present gardening frenzy? Their back-to-the-land, pure-food-and-water, free-love-in-the-grass (not just bluegrass and fescue, I might add) ideas were so seductive in the '60s. Why else would half the country have come to spend a huge majority of its leisure time on its knees in the garden if there weren't some revolutionary reason to do so?

And there were revolutionary reasons. The Hippies emerged following the '50s, the stiffest, smuggest decade of the century, not long after the end of the Second World War. People moved off the farms and into town, and then immediately fled the cities to build suburban tract houses the likes of which had never been seen. Madame was going to work in unprecedented numbers. Technology was burgeoning, and people found themselves with a dishwasher and lots more of something called Leisure Time. They bought TVS. They drove longer distances to the store. They discovered cookouts

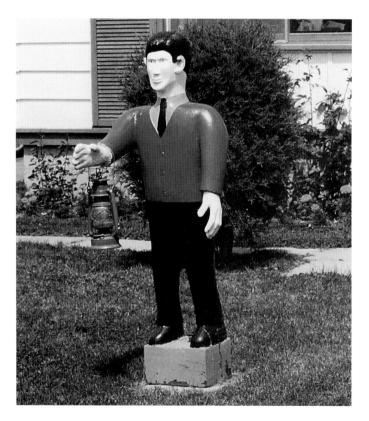

and back-yard swimming pools. They put swings and teeter-totters, which before then were found only in public parks, in their own yards. Not only did they move out of town, they also moved out of doors.

Then came the '60s, and suddenly students were rioting all over the world; there was a drug revolution; there was a racial revolution; there was a war in Vietnam and there was the FLQ. There was a sexual revolution, a women's revolution and a music revolution. To get away from all this, cultivating the garden seemed like the thing to do. When it caught on, it became a garden revolution that hasn't stopped till the present day.

There was more to it than that though. Time, land and money are at the root of this gardening madness, but there's also four thousand years of gardening tradition pushing us outdoors too. *Tradition*, as in folk art? Hold on to your sun bonnets; here we go again.

The Garden's Beginnings

The Western concept of the garden almost always starts with the Garden of Eden, and if ever there was a word that says "garden," it's "Eden." Adam, Eve, every known plant and animal in the world—a lush paradise story told and recognized by Christian and non-Christian alike.

"Paradise" is from the Greek word *paradeisos,* meaning "garden" or "orchard." And *paradeisos* had Persian roots, a proto-Iranian combination of words that meant "enclosed park." Given that geographical location, this would have put Eden right in the Fertile Crescent.

In the second chapter of *Genesis,* when God made Eden and filled it with people, plants and animals, he also created a river "to water the garden" and then divided the river into four parts. Two of these rivers are the Tigris and the Euphrates. For centuries, people believed that the Garden of Eden really existed, and that it was probably located in the Fertile Crescent somewhere between the Tigris and Euphrates Rivers. They also believed they would find it if they looked long and hard enough. But after centuries of unsuccessful search in Persia, they decided Eden must be elsewhere.

Facing page: Arthur Erwin made several lawn figures, but none with more charm then this formally dressed sidewalk light. The Lantern Bearer, as he is affectionately known, is related to the jockey-and-groom tradition of front-lawn statuary. Winchester, Ontario. (Wes Mattie. CMC 80-401)

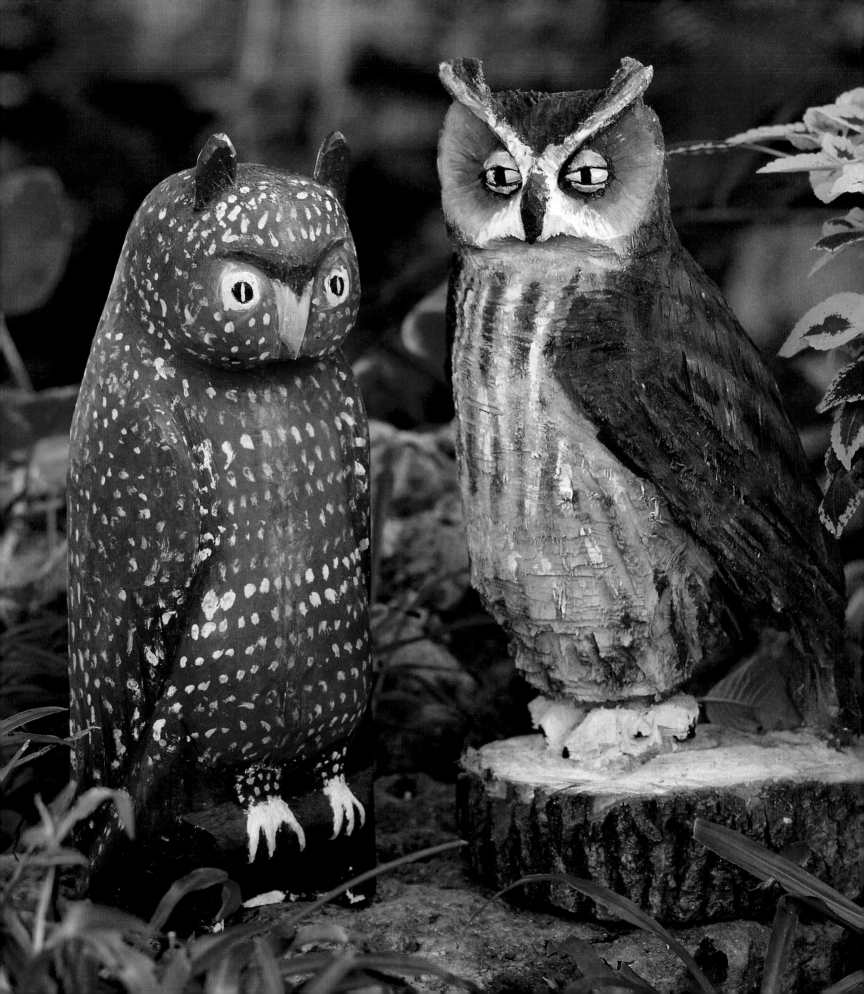

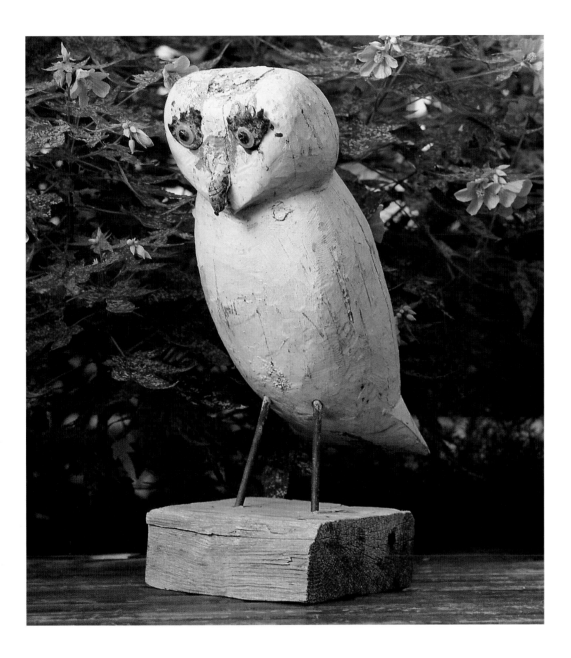

A thoroughly anonymous owl, who wisely keeps his own counsel.
(Harry Foster; CMC 79-1721)

Facing page: Field mice, we know where you live! Collins Eisenhauer's
brown owl [left], with its cleverly painted feet, hunches next to Ron
Barber's more calculating specimen [right]. Mr. Barber, of Orono, Ontario,
roughed out his carving with a chainsaw before finishing and painting.
(Harry Foster; Eisenhauer piece: CMC 77-274; Barber: CMC 80-93)

Legend has it that Columbus was looking for it in the New World, and
early Western European botanists tried to recreate it by bringing home plant
samples from around the globe.

If the Garden of Eden wasn't in the Fertile Crescent, what was? The
Hanging Gardens of Babylon made a good substitute for quite a while. In
600 B.C., or so the story goes, King Nebuchadnezzar married a young
woman who was not from his neighbourhood in Babylon. She missed the
mountains where she was born, so Nebuchadnezzar, who had time, leisure
and money, set about making a huge, artificial mountain for her, including
terraces dripping with lush plants, running streams and shade trees.
It was so extraordinary, the Greeks awarded it one of the highly coveted
Seven Wonders of the World awards.

Trouble was, the award came five centuries after the Hanging Gardens
had been built, and they had apparently disappeared back into the landscape.
But true or not, Greek historians described the gardens at length, probably
based on some of those folk legends. (Folk legends are often accurate.
Heinrich Schliemann, the amateur German archaeologist, found Troy after a
careful reading of Homer's version of similar legends; and recent scholarship
indicates that the Garden of Eden may in fact have been on the then lush
island of Bahrain, just east of the Syrian desert.)

Whatever the truth, the Garden of Eden and the Hanging Gardens
of Babylon are the starting points that eventually bring us to our own garden
at the corner of Maple and Main. They will help create the setting where
we may place our own home-grown folk art.

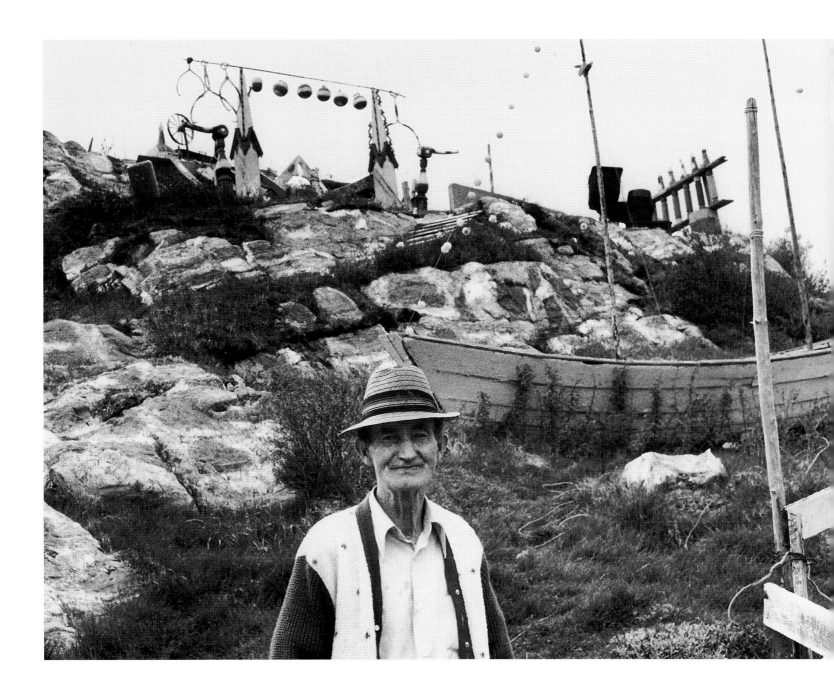

John Coady stands in front of his famous "Coady's Mountain."
The mountain was covered with folk art of all types, and the rocks were
painted every colour imaginable. Cape Broyle, Newfoundland.
(Wes Mattie)

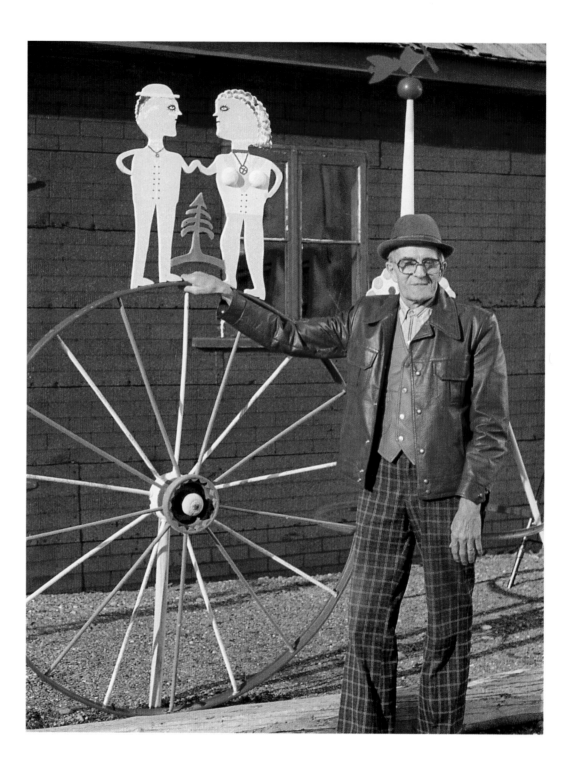

Gardens in Egypt, Greece and Rome

Around the north and south shores of the Mediterranean, garden traditions were growing at different rates and with different emphases—many of which would eventually influence gardening in Canada.

Although there is no direct archaeological evidence of ancient Egyptian gardens, there seems to be ample written, or in this case, drawn evidence that gardens were built and used. Among the extraordinary mass of burial items dating from a full thousand years before Christ that have come to us from Egypt are paintings of "walled gardens" attached to the dwellings of the period. Vegetables and fruits are distinctly depicted, as well as shade trees or vines overhead. Reclining benches are also apparent, as is a very clear water source, in one case containing both fish and ducks.

Most interesting is that some of the artistic decorations in the garden structure seem to be crop related. Native plants such as the lotus are portrayed on roof columns and houseposts. It is perhaps too early to even think about folk art in the garden, but there's no reason it shouldn't be there, given the urge to personalize outdoor space.

Turning to Greece, we have much better luck with statuary and art in the outdoor environment, but less luck with garden history. Of course, we do know that many houses in Greek cities had small, central courtyards serving several families, where fruit and vegetables could be grown. We can also deduce that the ancient Greeks were among the first to develop city parks, playgrounds and playing fields. These were spaces reserved for the gathering

Facing page: A prolific folk artist, Alphonse Grenier stands proudly with "Adam and Eve" in his personal Garden of Eden in Saint-Jean-de-la-Lande, Quebec, 1978. (Wes Mattie; CMC 80-133)

of people for political activities, military exercises and sport. When trees were planted, these became places to sit in the shade and chat, discuss and debate. In a very real way, they were not unlike the village greens and town squares we still see in modern Greece and on our own continent.

We also know that the Greeks loved statuary, and since there were temples and public buildings everywhere, there were also plenty of statues, undoubtedly including both fine and folk art. Thus while the concept of the private garden may not have been fully developed in classical Greece, the public garden was well known, used and decorated in a fashion that won't, I hope, surprise us at this stage.

In classical Rome, the situation was slightly different. Italy was not quite as arid as Greece, and in many areas the landscape was less perpendicular. Living outdoors was therefore a good deal more agreeable. Roman architecture lent itself perfectly to this sort of climate, and a large walled garden was often attached to even modest homes. Walls were sometimes painted with outdoor scenes, and statuary and other forms of decoration, such as tiled mosaics on the floor, were placed at intervals.

The Romans were excellent plumbers, so there was water in each home. Fountains and pools of various descriptions could be included in gardens of almost any size, and plant cultivation was natural. Vines were frequently trained overhead, creating shady corners where one could take a glass of wine at leisure.

We know all this, incidentally, because Pompeii and Herculaneum were preserved almost intact after Vesuvius erupted unexpectedly. Come to think about it, I myself have sipped wine in an Italian garden in Ottawa that also met all the criteria I've just listed. This maintenance of tradition is to be expected, given the strength of traditions.

One more thing about Rome. The Romans, it seems, invented the cottage. Since there was little space in the cities for growing vegetables, those who could afford it had a villa outside the city where a real food garden could be properly maintained. Very rich citizens had yet another villa for pure relaxation. These latter structures often boasted flower gardens, the first noted directly by historians. Incidentally, the art of topiary was refined by Roman green-thumbs; trees and shrubs were clipped and shaped into geometric or other sculptural shapes. This art—possibly a folk art—was effectively lost until the nineteenth century, but seems to be on the rise again judging by observations here in Canada. Pre-shaped, live topiary can be found for sale in garden centres, and garden and specialty catalogues offer artificial, fully leafed topiary in fiberglass containers, selling for about four hundred Canadian liras a piece!

The Islamic Garden

The biblical story of God putting a river into the Garden of Eden and dividing it into four smaller rivers is known to Muslims as well as Christians, and the four flowing streams have become the basis for most Islamic gardens.

Since water was so incredibly precious in the centre of the Muslim world, those four rivers still flow symbolically in a traditional Muslim garden, usually dividing the garden into four equal parts from a central pool or fountain.

Each channel leading away from the centre was frequently lined with blue tile to reflect the sky, giving the impression of added depth and lending colour to the surrounding courtyard.

How did the Islamic gardening tradition come to the West? First, the Crusaders came back to Europe steeped in Muslim customs, even though they had gone east to fight the Infidel. Second, Islam spread all across the southern shores of the Mediterranean Sea and with the Moors right up into Spain. The enclosed garden with its four water courses can still be seen in such major palaces as the famous Alhambra. Much of this tradition then came to Mexico with the Spanish and thus into the southwestern United States, influencing an entire generation of California landscape architects who wrote much of the book for twentieth-century gardening across North America. In Canadian gardens, indeed, the "water feature," as landscape architects are fond of calling it, remains an essential component of the complete garden.

Of course, Canadian gardeners are not dogmatic on the subject of the four courses of the river, but we persist in wells (stylized wishing wells if we have no actual water), ponds, swimming pools, wading pools, hot tubs, fountains and birdbaths—all symbolic water sources that spell nature to us in a very special way. Who would have thought that all this desire for water in the garden may have come directly from the desert?

As for folk art in the Muslim garden, the Koran forbade portraits and statuary. However, the Muslims' splendid geometric designs, made by arguably the best mathematicians in the then known world, resonated in many later gardening traditions.

Facing page: A handful of takes on garden decoration: a bathtub shrine to the Virgin Mary and a Hallowe'en witch from Ontario; a ranch gate and yard filled with birdhouses and whiligigs from Nova Scotia; and two pieces of lawn statuary—a Virgin with pink flamingo from Alberta, and a Quebec chicken planter. In each case the artist has achieved the goal of creating "something different." (Phil Tilney and Wes Mattie)

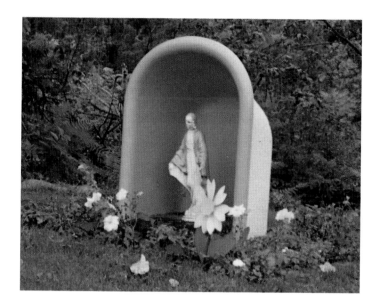

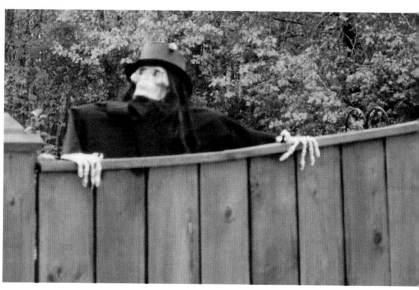

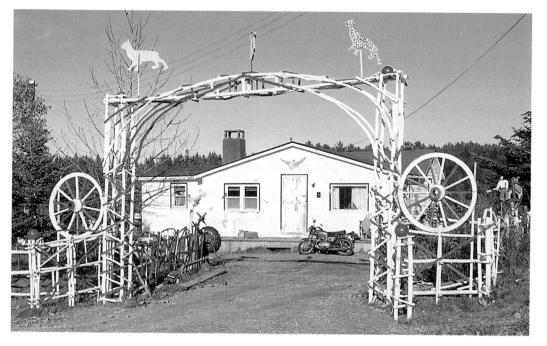

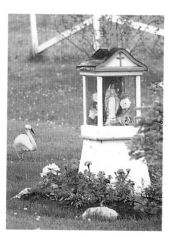

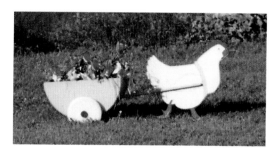

The Medieval Garden

The European medieval garden owes a great deal to the Islamic model. Once again, the enclosed garden included an important water feature, as well as the geometric cross motif in the centre—usually four walking paths instead of water courses. Obviously, the religious overtones were more Christian than Muslim, and many of the best examples were in fact found in monasteries or in the attached cloisters.

While the monasteries and convents were the centres of Christianity, they were also centres of scholarship where books were preserved and monks tirelessly copied what written knowledge survived. The inner garden came to be known as the *hortus conclusus,* the enclosed garden, and the feelings of safety this protected enclave provided played both to religion and intellect. The *hortus conclusus* was thought to be feminine in nature, much like a woman's womb, and thus the Virgin Mary was frequently invoked. This was a paradise on Earth, another Eden.

Medieval gardens give us another clue about our own designs. In the Middle Ages, grass began to be grown as a garden feature. Steps and benches of turf became well known. Mind you, we had to wait until the mid nineteenth century for the invention of a good lawnmower, but lawn science was already well under way. The preferred medieval method for killing weeds in the lawn was to pour boiling water on them, an environmentally friendly method we might think of reviving. A small variety of statuary, much of it religious, could be found within the garden. Other decorations were architectural in nature, incorporated into the walls and doorways.

It may be stretching it to say that the cookout originated within the cloistered walls of the medieval gardens, but dining did take place here, as did dancing, strolling in couples and various games and amusements. In fact, many Canadian back-yard activities certainly have origins in this enclosed area.

Outside the walls of the medieval gardens, other developments were in process that would speak to gardeners in later generations. Separate orchards were begun, an area of specialization for fruit. The same was true for vegetable gardens—set in separate walled spaces—and herb gardens, which were, after all, the source for much of the medicine of the period. At the same time, the villages that frequently sprang up in the shadow of the monasteries and castles began to develop small gardens attached to each home. These were more likely to be the locations for homemade art pieces. The incredible flowering of the Renaissance was about to begin.

European Renaissance Gardens

The exuberant Italian Renaissance garden drew on a variety of established norms and traditions and added its own creative high spirits—just as folk art did.

Renaissance garden designers drew from the Islamic traditions, incorporating water into their creations and also making gardens a part of the actual home. From the medieval cloister gardeners, they took the idea of linking several of these outdoor rooms together; and finally in accord with their Roman heritage, they incorporated the views of the landscape beyond the garden itself. (In Canadian terms, this means an enclosed back-yard

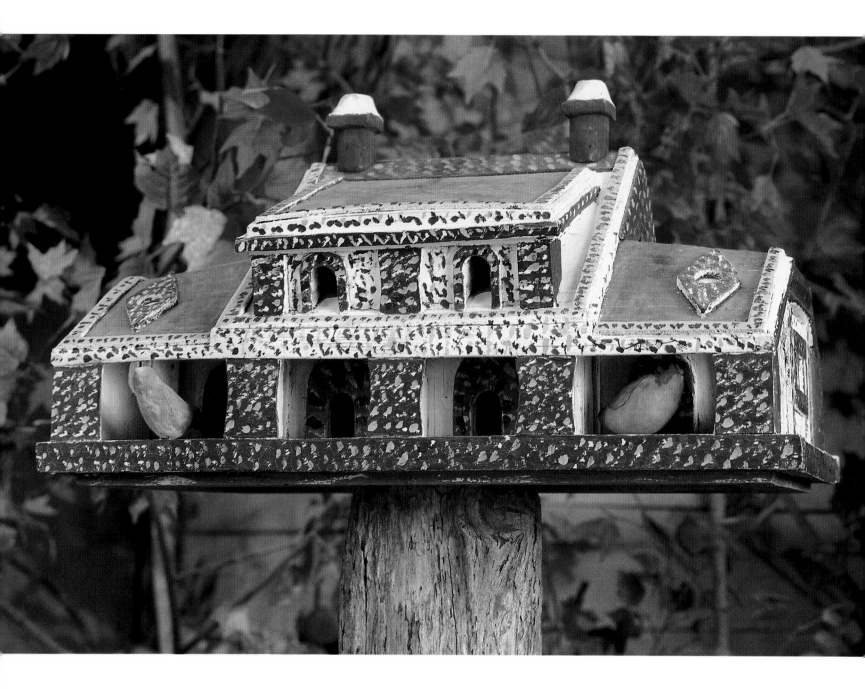

The dotted-paint technique, used by Charlie Atkinson of Cape Sable
Island, Nova Scotia, was used many places in Canada. Impressionistic in
tone, the technique here gives the effect of flowers climbing every wall of
the birdhouse. Note the two decoy birds hiding in the house's two side
doors. (Harry Foster; CMC 75-907)

deck for privacy; a pool or hot tub just beyond the hedge and a fantastic view of the lake, all connected by paths bordered with flowers and chosen pieces of outdoor art.) This is the period in which the use of outdoor statuary and three-dimensional art became popular. Renaissance garden architects added obelisks, urns, statuary, little buildings of every use and shape, trellises, spurting fountains, theatres, steps, gazebos, mazes, grottoes and more. It was literally a flowering of tangible outdoor art.

Suddenly, the variety of plants was bewildering. Alleys of trees led to walls with trained vines and fruit, presaging the French *espalier* tradition. A variety of colours filled the borders, and great attention was paid to scents. The sound of water was everywhere, and statuary and topiary animals were at every corner. In a very real sense, the French Canadian *patenteux* movement had its roots in this vigorous gardening and decorating practice. Both traditions loved a profusion of objects, vivid colours and crowds of fantastic creatures. Both exhibited a sense of theatre, astonishment and good humour.

The Renaissance revived the long-forgotten Roman custom of the Venus corner. In selected classical Roman gardens, a secret garden dedicated to the love goddess, Venus, was built, incorporating a reclining bench with a few surprisingly explicit statues. The idea was to take one's lady love there and let Nature take her course, as it were.

The Venus corner was part of the famous Renaissance tradition of *giochi d'acqua,* or water tricks. Water might spurt unexpectedly as strollers passed by, twirling heavenwards, even soaking them in the process. You may think that erotic or amusing water statuary had its final days in Renaissance Italy, but think for a moment about the famous statue in modern Brussels called *Manneken-Pis*—a representation of a little boy doing what comes naturally into a baroque fountain.

Think too of the wonderful Canadian wooden whirligig called "The Loving Couple," now in the Canadian Museum of Civilization in Ottawa. As it stood in its maker's front garden, it was a closed, white-painted box with a propeller whirling in the breeze. But when its owner opened it for privileged visitors, it revealed a naked man and woman locked in a loving and energetic embrace. Surely a worthy descendant of the Roman and Renaissance Venus corners of yore.

The Asian Connection

Long the symbol of the West's "discovery" of China, fourteenth-century traveller and trader Marco Polo, after his more than a dozen years in the East, brought back an astonishing number of descriptions of Chinese and Asian life. These included his stories of Chinese and even Japanese gardens.

Gardening in China was already well advanced by Marco Polo's time. But these were not the gardens of the ordinary people. In almost every province, emperors, landowners and a range of powerful figures had built gardens that were contemplative locations for meditation and appreciation of nature in microcosm.

In simple terms, the Taoists believed that every feature of nature had a spirit, and designing a garden presented a perfect opportunity to create a place where these spirits could dwell in harmony and serenity. This is, in fact an extremely complex endeavour, and there are details such as the direction and control of *ch'i*—the energy and life force present in all nature, including the air—which must be taken into account in the construction of a congenial garden. Through the science of *feng shui,* the garden builders knew exactly where to place the buildings, how to curve the water courses, and even where to erect the tree screens just inside the walls.

On my own visit to the Garden of the Humble Administrator in the southern Chinese city of Suzhou, I was astonished at the intricacy involved in both building and viewing a traditional Chinese garden. At almost every step, I was directed to see something entirely different from the previous view. Understanding the garden was an involved and thoughtful process. The Chinese meditative tradition is also reflected in our own garden uses. We turn to our gardens for serenity, for sunlight, for harmony with nature. Our traditions are certainly younger, but are just as meaningful.

In Japan, the dry Zen Buddhist garden is markedly different than the Taoist, although it has definite spiritual connection with its Chinese counterpart. Here, what we see as empty space actually has form and volume. The Zen garden is enclosed, with only a very few carefully selected boulders set in a bed of perfectly raked and patterned gravel. The raked gravel represents water, often a stream or small river. The large boulders represent land or islands. The gravel can be raked into different patterns, each to stimulate meditation and, ultimately, quiet revelation. Few if any plants are placed in the Zen garden, with the exception of fir trees, whose most important characteristic is that they do not change substantially with the seasons. That is the

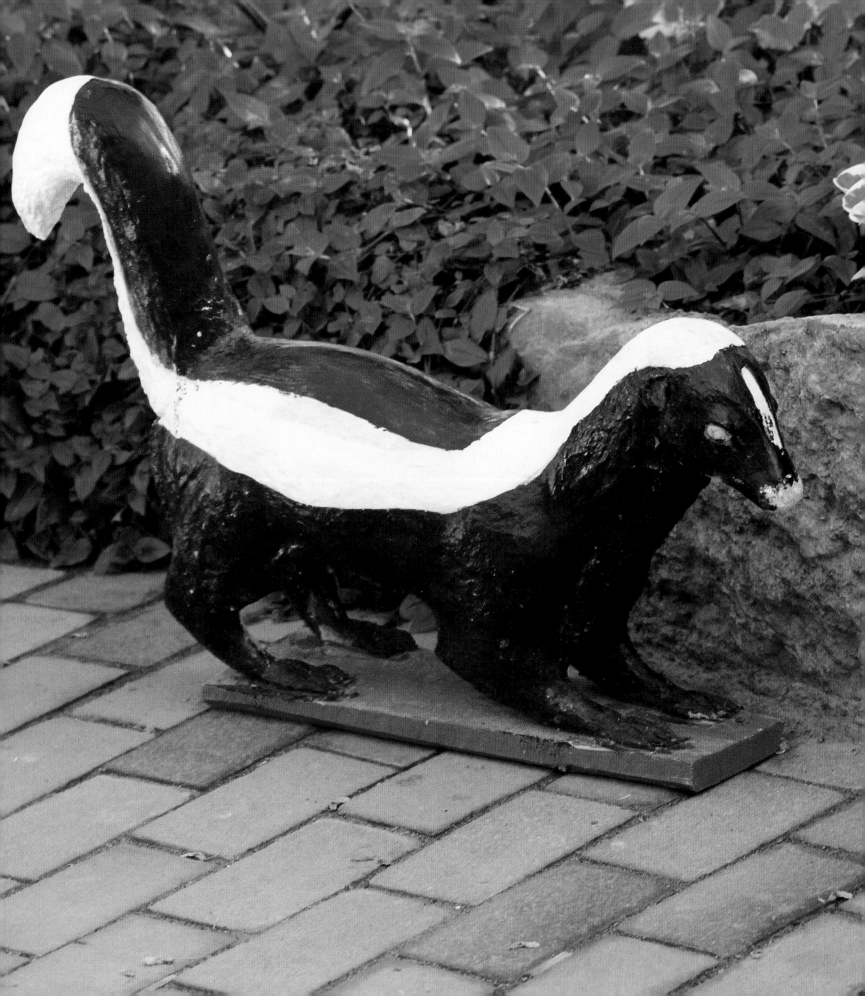

point. The Zen meditative garden reduces the garden space to absolute simplicity, only hinting at what might help in meditation with the ripples in the sand and the variously shaped rocks. One doesn't necessarily walk in this garden. Rather, one observes it as one would a quiet drama.

In the Canadian garden, we perhaps unintentionally use elements from both the Taoist and Zen traditions. We too have learned that nature abhors a straight line, and our gravel walks now curve, as do our flower beds. We endeavour to place our trees and lower plantings to complement the position of the garden and the house. We sit on our decks in the same way the Humble Administrator might have sat on his verandah. We may not consciously think, "Now, that's the way they might do it in a Taoist garden," but the same impetus is there.

As to Zen influences in a Canadian garden, don't scoff yet. How many times have you seen an enormous rock on a front lawn, often planted round with impatiens and marigolds, perhaps sporting a pink flamingo for contrast? To be sure, the boulder might have come out of the cellar hole and the owner couldn't be bothered to move it, but it has become a centre-point that draws the eye and may save the property from rigid symmetry.

There are other, genuinely Canadian uses of rocks. In 1974 Pierre Théberge, the present director of the National Gallery of Canada, spotted a superb series of painted rocks in the driveway of one Arthème St. Germain on a farm west of Hull, Quebec. After many weeks of quiet negotiation, Théberge managed to acquire the rocks and stored them and many other examples

Facing page: Nettie Sharpe, the prolific Quebec folk art collector, named "Bellodgin," the skunk, after a famous 1920s perfume. Very few folk art carvings acquire names, so characters such as Bellodgin, Clem the scarecrow and Ti-Gus the truncated man in the red uniform must hold the particular affection of their owners and collectors. (Harry Foster; CMC 77-956)

of St. Germain's folk art in his own apartment. The National Gallery's curatorial staff finally refused the rocks on the grounds that they were probably folk art and the gallery dealt primarily in fine art.

Théberge and Greg Curnoe, one of Canada's wonderful fine artists, deceased at a tragically early age, formed a society called *The Association for the Documentation of Neglected Aspects of the Culture of Canada*. With a spirited defence for the acquisition of such objects in the first and only issue of their society's journal, they succeeded in placing the rocks with the Museum of Man, now the Canadian Museum of Civilization. They were among the first of the effusive representatives of Quebec's *patenteux*. Rocks are important not *only* in dry Zen situations. Our folk art painted rocks too have symbolic value. They clearly give to those who make them a sense of self and of home. They individualize space with a kind of visual address, different from every other, yet at the core, the same.

The French and English Gardeners Come to Canada

The Italian Renaissance effectively made gardening spirited again, but the French gardeners refined it. The seventeenth century saw the development of truly formal gardens, perfect geometric shapes that could be viewed with satisfaction from the upper stories of the chateau, their owners confident that weeds (and the lower classes) were kept at bay.

The triumph of this style can still be seen today in the astonishing gardens of the palace of Versailles. This unutterably huge complex of gardens, kilometres of walkways, lengthy reflecting pools, playing fountains and streets full of sculpture (not exactly folk art, but in the same spirit!) was the triumph of French landscape architect André Lenôtre, working for the Sun King himself, Louis XIV.

It took almost half the century to build Versailles, with its parterre, knee-high hedges and its paths of crushed rock in different colours and textures. Sadly, apart from a few echoes in Britain in the following century, this style of gardening did not endure. Man's place in nature was being reassessed. It was a French philosopher, Jean-Jacques Rousseau, who was at least partly responsible. The Noble Savage and the birth of romanticism were just around the corner, and a more flowing and flowery style of gardening—much the same one we still enjoy—would take over.

In eighteenth-century Britain, revolutionary garden designers such as Humphrey Repton and the remarkable Lancelot "Capability" Brown began to convince their rich and landed clients to dispense with symmetry, square pools and perfectly clipped topiary. Instead they urged irregularly shaped water courses, trees and shrubs growing in gentle curves right down to the lake shoreline, lawns, glades and a surprise for the eye around every corner.

"Capability" Brown's clients were noble landowners whose gardens and grounds remain today not only as monuments to an age, but also as the single heaviest influence on landscaping techniques for both the nineteenth and twentieth centuries, and probably beyond. His influence was eclipsed—enhanced really—only by the famous nineteenth-century English garden designer Gertrude Jekyll. Jekyll's work, in fact, really spanned both the nineteenth and twentieth centuries. She and her colleague, architect Sir Edwin

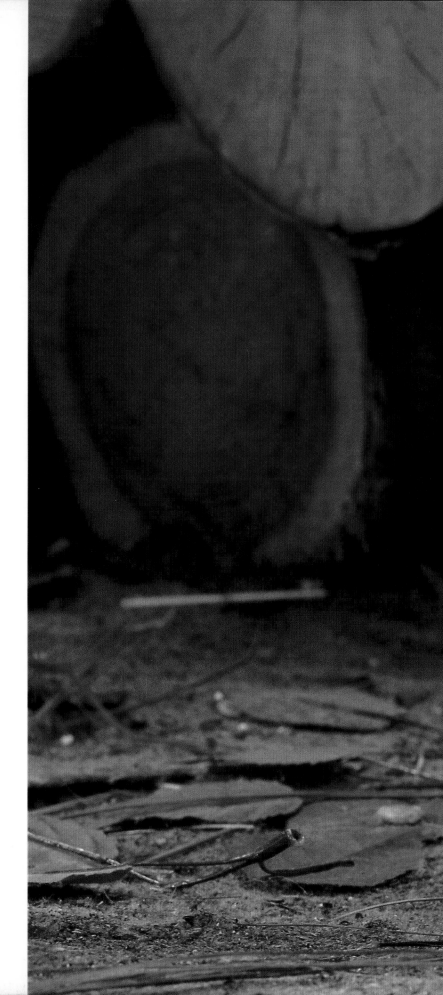

Antonio Matteo, an Italian
immigrant now living in Montreal,
carved a series of splendidly
coloured outdoor creatures.
This contemplative rooster with
his incised coxcomb sports
feathers worthy of the pointillist
painting tradition of the early
impressionists. (Harry Foster;
CMC 94-814)

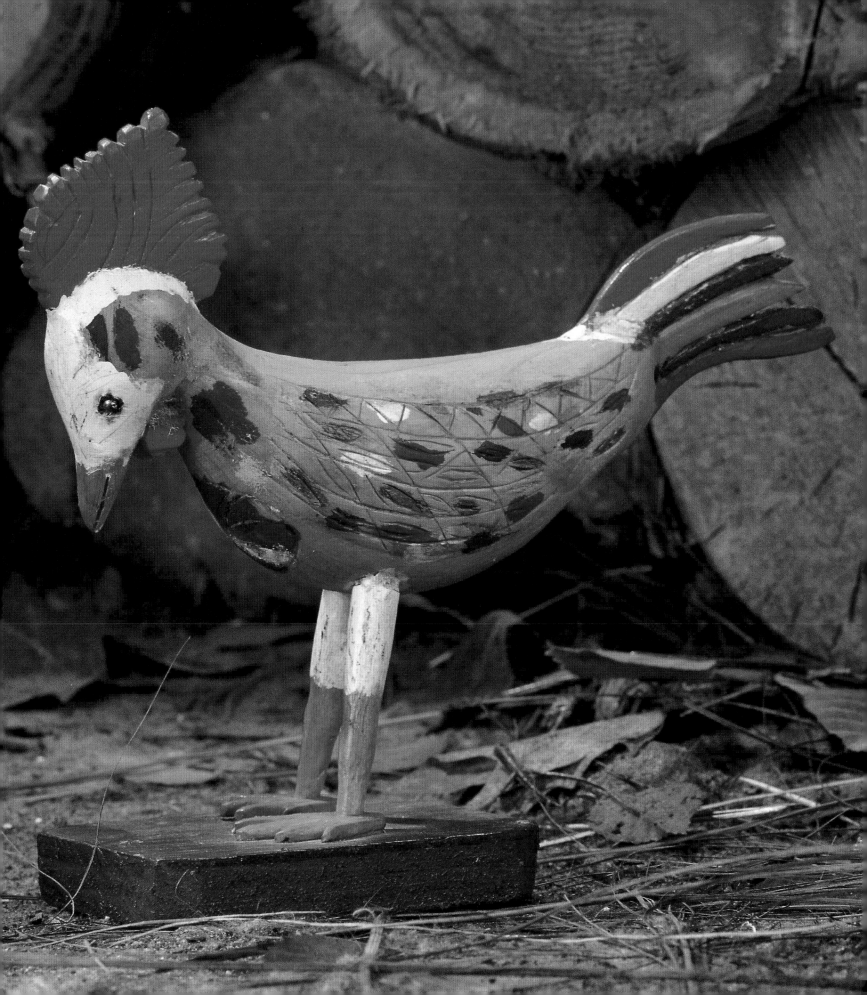

Lutyens, designed residences with soft, almost impressionist gardens, colours flowing one over the other as English gardens seem to do today. Indeed, Jekyll was a painter before she became a landscape gardener, and the story is told that when she developed serious eye trouble, her garden designs came to reflect her blurred vision. Nevertheless, it is Jekyll's designs that carry on in the English garden and which have crossed the Atlantic to find a place in many Canadian gardens as well.

The French and English influences in Canadian gardens have been apparent from the earliest days of this country. Like the weatherlore the settlers brought along in their memories, knowledge of how gardens "should" be constructed and decorated with period art came along with them too. This knowledge included much of the history we have already discussed but was moulded to the Canadian landscape, climate and all the conditions brought on by moving to a new land—to say nothing of hacking out garden space from virgin forest, in many cases!

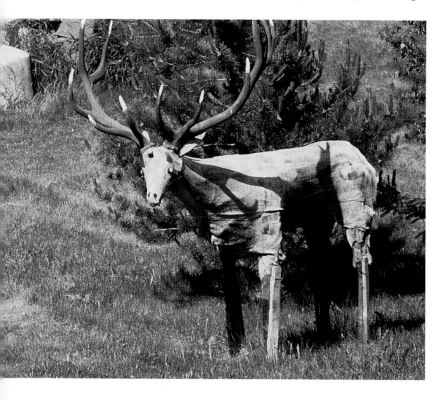

Early Canadian gardens were of course small, and dedicated to survival. Once food and shelter were more or less assured, flower gardens could blossom as well, but usually in strictly enclosed spaces. Houses built directly on the street had no room for front lawns, but a few herbs might have found a place by selected doorsteps. Some herbs, such as lavender or chives, bloom gloriously and would have been considered useful as well as aesthetic. If you see a parallel here between plants grown in the garden and the development of folk art, it is no accident. In both developments, the useful predominated, followed by a combination of the utilitarian mixed with the eye-catching. It is also fair to say that both fine art and the art of landscaping have their respective superstars, some of whose ideas inevitably percolate to home-based artists and gardeners, who in turn adapt those professional ideas. It's as if folk artists and back-yard gardeners work on a remarkably similar wavelength. But even though this percolation does take place, the reality of the Canadian landscape and the individual attitudes of her artists helped develop unique directions as well.

As time allowed and as houses grew in size, miniature gardens modelled on the great estates began to be planted and cultivated. Gardening handbooks were always available, and the writings of nineteenth-century North American landscape stars such as Andrew Jackson Downing or Frederick Law Olmsted not only influenced the layout of towns and cities but also individual landscapes within them. Downing wrote widely read gardeners' "how to" books, telling moneyed landowners how the North American landscape could be turned into proper residences with model gardens. Olmsted is probably best known for his mid-nineteenth century design of Central Park in New York City, where he literally moved (and built) mountains and created "natural" vistas, while allowing traffic to pass through virtually unnoticed. But his landscape and park designs are also found in a dozen other American cities and as far north as Montreal. Central Park and other triumphs made Olmsted's work a model for at least a century.

Facing page: A deer statue remains a commonplace of garden decoration. This folk art stag sports a real skull and twelve-point antlers; the body is made from sticks and recycled burlap feedbags. Made by Dave Gibson from Nevis, Alberta, 1975. (Wes Mattie)

Canada too had its landscape design stars, some of whom were trained in and were certainly influenced by both European and American traditions. Howard Grubb trained in England, but brought his knowledge to Canada in 1911. Grubb worked in tandem with his equally famous and professionally trained wife—a rarity before the First World War—Lorrie Alfreda Dunington. Well before it became fashionable in this country, they combined their names. Together, the pair of talented landscape architects created modern landscape design in Canada, and they became founding members of the Society of Canadian Landscape Architects in 1934. They were also, it is said parenthetically, a dynamic and delightful duo on the Toronto social circuit.

He saw the garden as a place of fantasy and delight, an escape valve from urban stress; hence his eclectic mix of international gardening traditions. She was an expert in flowers and the perennial garden, and between them they became the backbone of pre-Second World War beaux arts gardening and design development. Some of their work—both public and private— still survives. Although Lorrie Dunington-Grubb died in 1944, Howard continued to work until his own death in 1965. On your next visit to University Avenue in Toronto, look at the carefully designed and planted mall that divides the north and south roadways. This is the later work of Howard Dunington-Grubb.

Equal in influence, albeit postwar and on Canada's west coast, is the remarkable teamwork of architect Arthur Erickson and landscape architect Cornelia Hahn Oberlander. In much the same way Lutyens and Jekyll

Facing page: Alcide St. Germain's version of the dotted-paint technique, this time on a two-foot-high peacock with a beady eye and splendid pink feet. (Harry Foster; CMC 80-156)

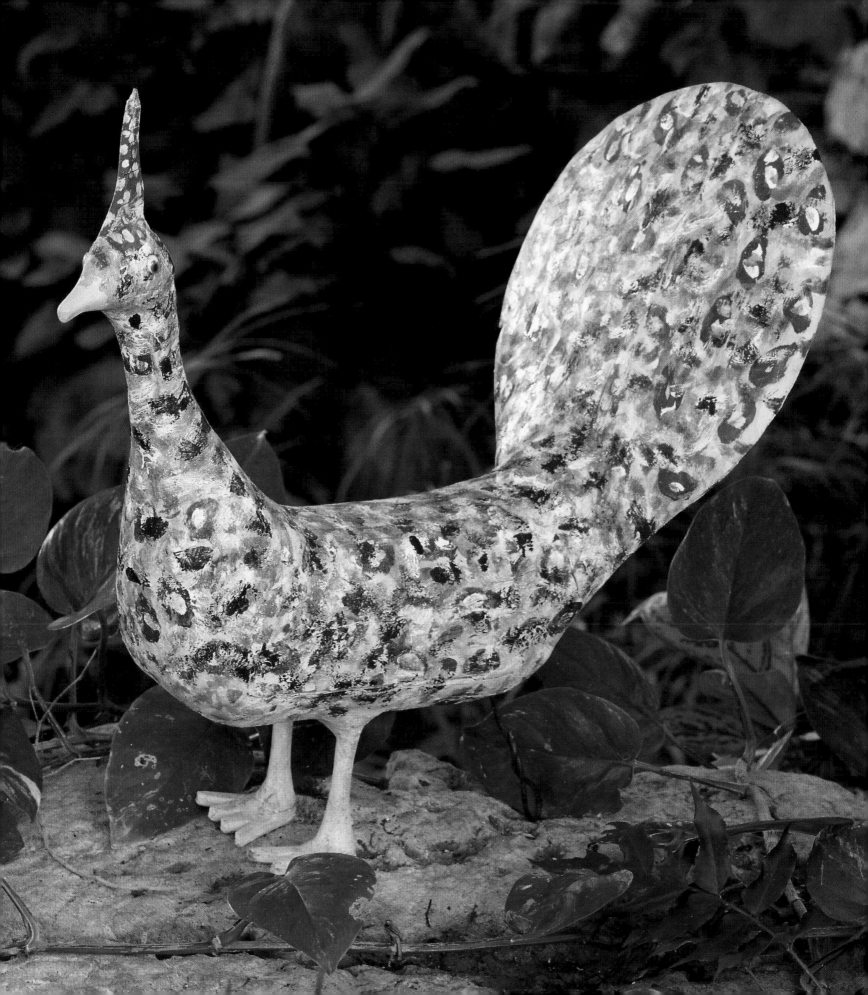

collaborated on English residences and public grounds, Erickson and Oberlander's work remains as some of Canada's most interesting and influential. Both members of the team are always vitally interested in the natural contours of a site and how the building, landscape design and plantings should work with their context. Two particularly well-known public Erickson-Oberlander collaborations are Vancouver's Robson Square and the new Canadian Chancery in Washington, D.C. Ideas from these and many other influential landscape architects and gardening experts have found their way into the Canadian gardens, parks and greenscapes of today.

While these well-documented garden "movements" predominated, it is also probably fair to say that the gardens and lawns we take for granted today really did not become popular in Canada until well after the First World War. Village greens and open spaces were not the clipped greenswards we admire today. Rather, these were often muddy storage dumps, places where grazing animals were allowed or even encouraged to roam, and where well-worn footpaths wound across from store to town hall. Streets also were muddy; tall grass, weeds and shrubs predominated between roadway and front porch. "Foundation plantings" literally hid the stark foundations of houses; and walkways, if any, went arrow-straight from street to steps. Hardly anyone worked only forty hours a week, so the time required for more than subsistence gardening and right-angle design really did not exist. Although spacious lawns were developed in Britain in the eighteenth century, and although lawn mowers were perfected in the 1860s, the concept, indeed, the mind-set of the lawn and garden came to middle-class Canada much later.

It was only with the advent of the automobile, more regulated working hours, child labour laws and a host of other social reforms that the Canadian garden as we know it today began to emerge. The lawn, set back from the road by the sidewalk, could now be trimmed and bordered with flowers. The "stage" was set not only for the Canadian garden, including its public front lawn and its more private back yard, but also for the flowering of three-dimensional decorations—including folk art—which was yet to come.

After the Second World War and into the 1950s, suburbia began to emerge. Pride in our grounds combined with conformist pressure to keep it all tidy. Yet the urge to create and the time to do it finally showed up in the garden. Folk art, the quiet appreciation of a handy, beautiful thing, with the possible additional impetus of folk tradition behind it, came out the door and became a splendour in the grass. For thirty years, outdoor folk art was a cultural phenomenon to view, to inform, to delight and, finally, to wither and disappear.

What has taken its place and where do we go from here? We'll take one last glance at the garden of today, and then look to the future of folk art in the next chapter.

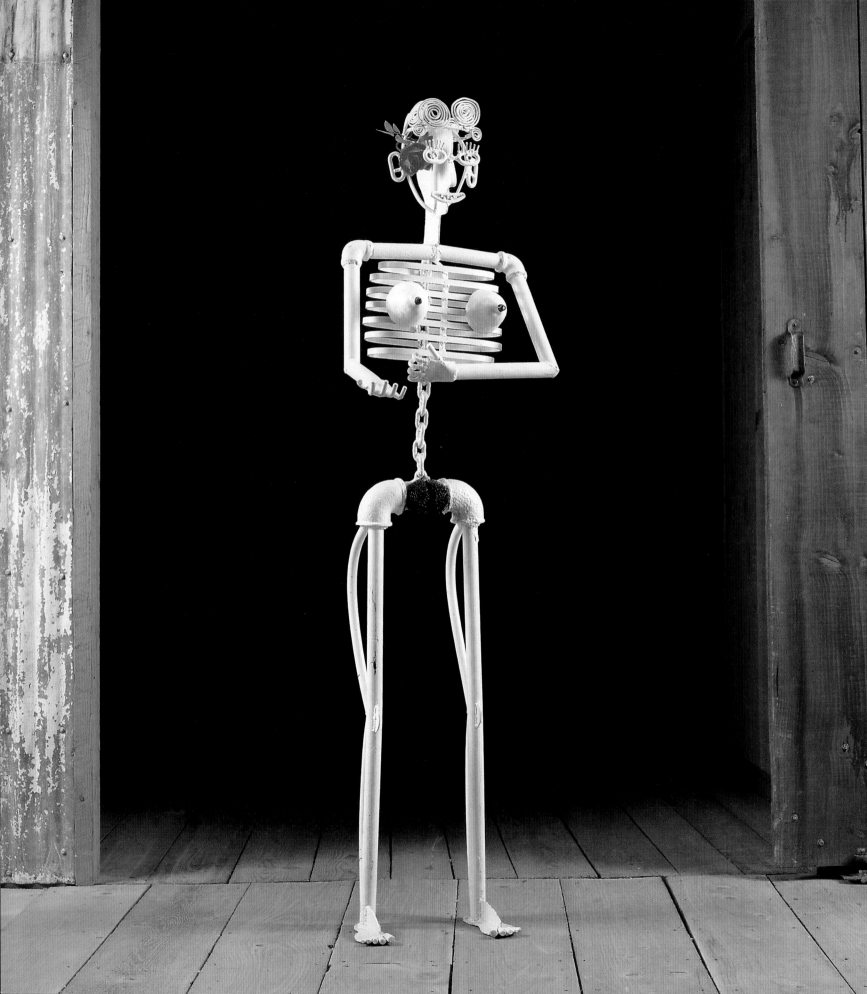

The Morphing of Folk Art and the Canadian Garden

THE FOLK ARE NOT SENTIMENTAL; they are always one step ahead. As much as social scientists and others hope they can predict how people will think and act, we the people—bless us—are always ready with a surprise.

In the blossoming, ebullient period of outdoor folk art in the latter half of the twentieth century, it seemed as if nothing could stop the avalanche of creativity. People designed, devised and decorated; other people bought, sold and collected. Still others observed, studied and analyzed. And yet, as we

Facing page: This skeletal woman is only one of many metal sculptures Albert Winje made on his Alberta farm. A talented metalworker and devoted recycler, Mr. Winje's people held coffee pots and sported hats and delicately placed tufts of steel wool. His people were always life size and remarkably eye catching. (Harry Foster; CMC 83-1714)

all saw, the folk surprised us. Outdoor folk art simply petered out at the end of the '80s. Something had to fill the vacuum left by its absence.

It was commerce. A person could go to White Rose, Michael's or Wal-Mart and pay less for a faux-folk lawn decoration than it would cost to make a good one at home, in money or time. Plastic whirligigs were there; bird houses—ready-made or to be assembled; statuary of every possible type; humorous, serious, tacky or tasteful, it was all for sale. Besides, the gnomes were better made, there was a choice between rubber, plastic or cement, and who would sit home sewing a flag that said "Twick or Tweet?" when you

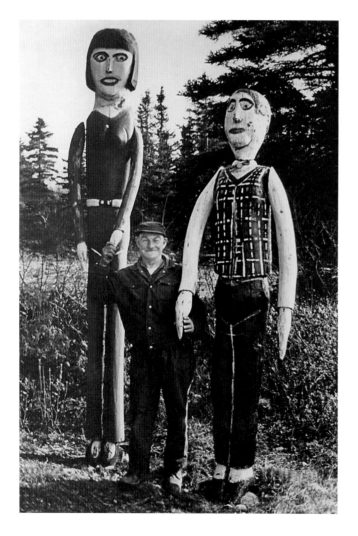

could buy a weatherproof one at a discount price? There are two more questions for those of us resisting such change with every fibre of our being. Remember the heart-warming stories of old-time Christmas trees with oranges, pine cones and home-made ornaments, and how unspeakably wonderful they were? What percentage of handmade ornaments do we find on our holiday trees today? There is a lesson here for both folk art and for gardens.

However, there were still several things that did not change in our gardens. The urge to decorate re-mained. The impulse to make a tangible performance on the front lawn did not change. The area between the house and the road was still a kind of magic space where highly embellished figures danced their well-proven routines. No longer were they painted with the over-bright hard-ware-store palette, but they were, as one lawn decorator told me repeatedly, "something different." This indeed was the magic. His lawn was different from the lawn next door; it was personal; it was individual; it was unique.

And therefore, so was he.

Never mind that the houses on the street were substantially the same; never mind that the cars and pick-ups on the street looked substantially the same. Or that the jobs, the schools and even the church might be the same for all the neighbours. At home, in his castle, he had created, and he was "something different."

Folk Art Outdoors

Some things are slower to change. Religion in the outdoors, for example. The Virgin Mary grotto remains (remember the *hortus conclusus?*), as do a variety of other saints and religious representations. Since the Second World War, Mary's grotto has been a cast-iron bathtub with four feet, turned vertical and planted in the garden. It was a perfect reminder of the Lourdes phenom-enon of 1858 when St. Bernadette had her repeated visions of the Virgin Mary. Reuse of the out-of-date bathtub, of course, was also a pinnacle of recycling, and using found objects for outdoor folk art falls well within acceptable limits. The "Virgin on the Half Shell," as she is rudely but widely known, can still be found in a great variety of side gardens. She is rarely a performance piece to be placed front and centre. More recently, cast concrete Virgins have become common; indeed precast grottoes are sold in many

Facing page: Folk artist Sidney Howard stands between two of his huge garden figures, made from discarded telephone poles. Mr. Howard added arms and heads with smiles that matched his own. Cape Breton, Nova Scotia. (Wes Mattie)

garden centres. There are even variations on a theme with the grotto shaped like two praying hands. St. Bernadette can also be bought in cast concrete, but not painted in the same traditional bright blue as the Holy Mother.

The wayside crosses of French Canada have a long history. Some of these large outdoor pieces served as shrines, built to commemorate local people or events. Others celebrated favours asked from or granted by a saint, while still others were talismans against natural disasters such as lightning or storms. Wayside crosses continue to be common, although one notices that as they fall down, they are less frequently replaced today. Some were natural platforms for traditional outdoor folk art and decoration. Many of the roosters mounted on the top of these sometimes massive structures, for example, have long since disappeared into the hands of pickers and antique lovers of all sorts. St. Francis appears in modern yard art collections, often in conjunction with a bird-feeding station. Joseph and Jesus, of course, and other saints occupy today's lawn shrines as well. At Christmas time, the crèche with the entire cast of characters has become a favourite. The magic of the garden still includes religion, apparently.

But there are other, more noticeable changes. Nonreligious seasonal decorations are beginning to assume major importance, first in stores, and later in front gardens. The hand-wrought evergreen Christmas wreaths of our immediate past gave way to plastic boughs woven in circles; these in turn changed into outdoor strings of lights and Frosty the Snowman with a light bulb in his tummy. In certain front yards, the full secular extravaganza of Santa, Rudolph, the sleigh and eight other reindeer appears, sometimes

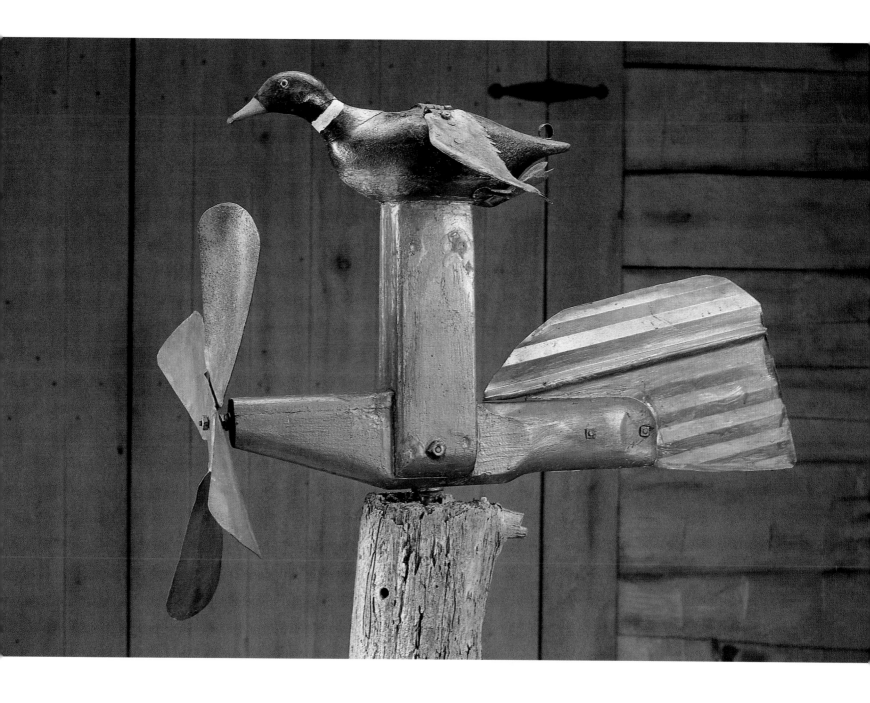

One of the loveliest whirligigs in the collection, Martin Yankovick's duck
(Kingston, Ontario, 1936) is exquisitely made and mechanically perfect.
Obviously, the clunky wind mechanism was secondary to the artist's
initial conception of the splendid mallard. (Harry Foster; CMC 83-1714)

seeming to move across the rooftops as the lights flash in sequence. And that may be only the appetizer. The main course might include an animated manger with nodding donkeys and noisy mechanical sheep.

Hallowe'en is now second only to Christmas as an occasion for outdoor decoration. The single carved jack-o'-lantern with a candle has been augmented by strings of orange lights strung across the façade of the castle. These are on sale well before Thanksgiving, although a few front-door turkeys may also be available for that particular holiday. Plastic spider webs hang in trees for the full month of October; graves appear in the grass, and ghosts fly in the shrubbery; bright orange leaf bags turn ghastly smiles on passers-by.

Harvest figures are starting to appear, possibly a wave of creativity from below the Canada–United States border, where such characters have been well-known for some years. These are usually pumpkin-headed figures with straw-stuffed clothes, perhaps further decorated with cornstalks and squash. More recently, the painted head and body armature can be had at discount

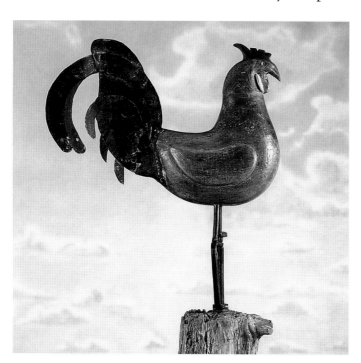

stores—you supply only your old jeans and stuff it with lawn clippings.

Snowmen, touched on above, and ice sculpture have gone well beyond the annual Carnival efforts in Quebec City. Now communities of every size have ice-sculpture tournaments, pitting professional ice-carvers (usually chefs) against talented amateurs. The ephemeral snowman has evolved into intricate snow families, some very well-dressed. For those living near a beach, sand sculpture is also claiming its share of attention. All have elements of a folk art tradition, yet their makers know they are as temporary as the tide or the January thaw.

Decorative door wreaths are seen now in any season, not just at Christmas. In spring, plastic daffodils woven into a circle appear on chosen front doors. In summer, these may be supplanted by a woman's straw gardening hat with ribbons and summer flowers. Fall can bring a straw wreath sporting plastic maple leaves in various shades of decay, all surrounded with yards of manufactured bittersweet vine. Valentine's Day has its strings of heart lights; Easter has its outdoor pastel egg trees. Only Canada Day seems stuck on a single, symbolic Canadian flag, although this is by no means universal.

None of this is bad or even tasteless. It is simply a collection of cultural facts that any one of us can observe during any given season. Of course, having observed this cascade of commerce, the natural question is what's next? Because "surprise" is the operative element here, we obviously do not know. But we can perhaps see signs.

Folklore has changed—one hesitates to use the word "morphed," but perhaps it fits the times. Folklore and folk art have morphed into other expressions of creativity or perhaps other systems of delivery. Anonymous oral folklore, for example, has moved part and parcel to the Internet. Jokes and oral expressions are still widely known, invented and told, but cyberspace is certainly the prime vehicle for transmission.

For folk art, think in terms personal expression. A whole generation is dyeing its hair in colours never before seen on a human head. Eye-catching

Facing page: This noble rooster was originally placed at the peak of a wayside cross in Quebec. Although it clearly had religious overtones in that context, it is also a splendidly brash Chanticleer with its painted metal tail feathers and carved wooden body. (Harry Foster; CMC 77-943)

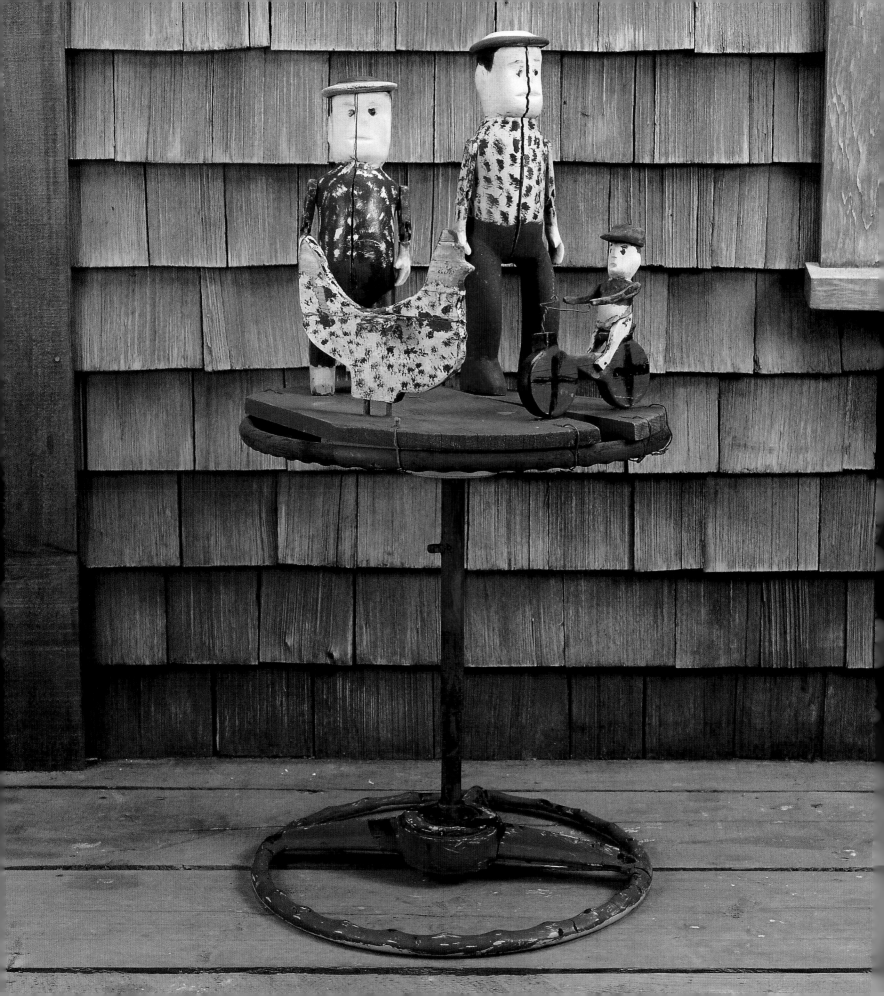

jewellery appears in places on the body many of us would blush to mention, much less observe. Even the geezer generation (that's mine) sees nothing strange in an executive in a three-piece suit who also sports a diamond stud or modest gold hoop earring.

The artistic canvas now includes the human hide. Tattoos, indeed, seem to push the envelope of folk art in a very real and rather interesting way. These drawings have a certain tradition (the pancultural history of tattooing is widespread and very ancient) and have an overlay of New Age and comic-book art. More important, they are personal expressions of an aesthetic impulse that stretches across many lines of society, age and gender. Tattoos are not just for sailors and bikers any more. Are tattoos folk art? Folk art has been "morphing," after all.

In this effort to aesthetically personalize ourselves and our surroundings, there are haircuts in which one's name, or that of one's team or sweetheart, can be "carved" into the close-cropped scalp. There is also the amazing variety of sneakers or telephones one may choose. Almost every person can look slightly "different," as the garden decorator said of his pink flamingoes and flock of sheep. Accessorizing takes on a slightly folk flavour.

Think, too, of personalized and unique coffee. New coffee shops—and there are many—have such a variety of options that a whole language has evolved to support unique personal expression. How about a short, decaf, amaretto latté with skim, not too hot, two and a half Sweet 'n Lows and a cinnamon stick on the side?

Facing page: Not exactly a whirligig, but not just a carving either, Ellison Eagles's use of two recycled steering wheels gives the two slightly vague figures a feeling of speed if not the reality. Their delicious deadpan expressions coupled with the tiny bicyclist and huge chicken make this one a favourite. North River, Ontario. (Harry Foster; CMC 79-1545)

The Garden in Transition

What about the garden? How will the traditions discussed here be changing in the future? For the middle class, the suburban house and its surrounding gardens are increasingly becoming things of the past. Modest high-rises and tight collections of garden homes are more the norm. Moshe Safdie's "Habitat" from Expo '67 may have foretold the future better than anyone realized. Pre-cast concrete rooms stacked in seemingly random but actually brilliant order have a certain draw. Every unit has light from different directions and an open-air porch (with room for very modest plantings), and the approach to every unit is slightly different from that of the neighbours. Personalized, unique space is incorporated right into a high-density design. What will happen to the gardening instinct in such an environment?

High-definition, flat-screen television is now a reality. Instead of a full-sized garden outdoors, can we not see a personal, private back-yard garden filling up one whole wall on a two-inch thick screen? Perspective is possible, and we could choose whatever style garden we wanted. The sun could come up and go down. It could actually rain. Fountains, paths, birds flying by—all feasible. Indeed, we could have a planting program and watch spring flowers emerge, followed by the summer annuals and, eventually, the fall foliage. We could even weed, fertilize and water by keyboard. And design and draw in outdoor art. We could erase and "regrow" the whole thing next week in a new configuration.

In the Canadian winter, a bright desert cactus garden on an entire wall would certainly warm the atmosphere indoors. Or a cool winter landscape might calm the brain on a blistering August afternoon. The possibilities are limitless. If this seems strange, I wonder how many besides myself have seen the Living Aquarium programs for personal computers? You select the fish and the plants; they must be fed and treated for disease; the "tank" must be cleaned; and yes, the fish occasionally die and have to be digitally removed. It is very similar to the Virtual Pet craze of recent times in which tiny, hand-held creatures piteously beeped when hungry, dirty or lonely. Perhaps we have already seen more of the future than we want to admit.

There will be other developments in the garden of the future. There has been talk of genetically altered grass that will not grow past a certain height. We already know of potatoes and other vegetables with built-in insecticides and weed repellers. Still other edibles are programed not to change colour so rapidly, giving them a longer shelf life. Even our lawn mowers are finding new occupations. One of the hottest new sports on the continent is lawn-mower racing. Proud owners pilot souped-up garden tractors with names such as Sodzilla, The Turfinator, Thatch 22 and The Lawn Ranger. No kidding.

In the waning summers of this millennium, baseball-stadium grounds-keepers have been vying for the most decorative and aesthetically interesting grass-cutting patterns. Some achieve gently curving parallel lines, others a crisp checkerboard or four-leafed clovers. This is landscaping made for television—mowing for the mind. The competition for viewer commentary is said to be intense. Mazes too have come back into fashion, both in contemplative institutions such as churches and as back-yard decorations.

Similarly, since the first space-men hoaxes were solved, making geometric designs in pristine fields of wheat has become a kind of personal-art sport, reported regularly in the press. All of these are gardening ideas with definite futures—perhaps best accomplished in the private gardens that still remain.

Finally, "guerrilla gardening" is becoming increasingly popular. For those who do not have gardens of their own, the desire to surreptitiously plant and nurture flowers or even vegetables on public property or forgotten bits of alleyway greenspace has become a national trend. Gardening and outdoor folk art, though both may be undergoing serious and deep changes, have certain, indefinable characteristics that keep us coming back to them. There is something utterly elemental about human hands in soil, planting seeds that actually come to life. The feeling this gives the gardener is something that cannot be duplicated with words, or text, or on a screen. Gardening, whether mutated or miniaturized or restricted to containers, will not disappear. Likewise with folk art; the urge to decorate and demarcate personal space is so ingrained, it too will not go away quietly.

In neither case can we make firm predictions. The folk artists and the gardeners are always one step ahead, and they will surprise us. The only constant in culture is change.

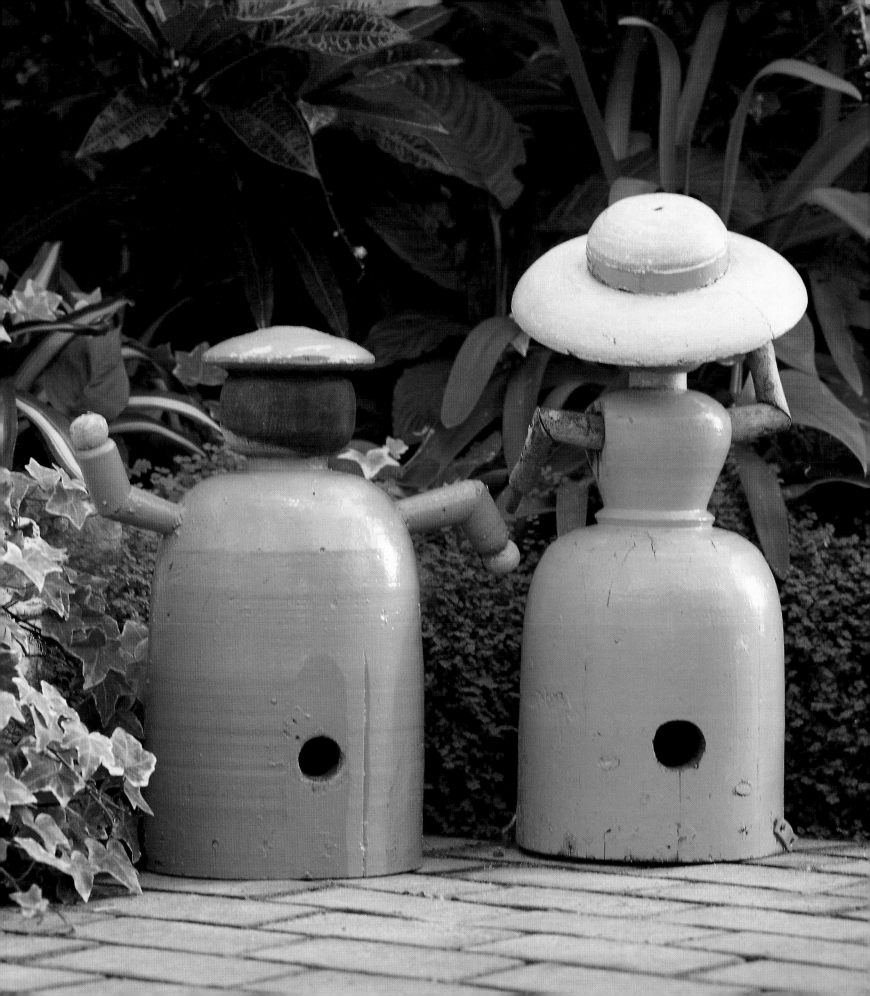

Bibliography

FOLKLORE

Bird, Michael, and Terry Kobayashi. *A Splendid Harvest: Germanic Folk and Decorative Arts in Canada.* Toronto: Van Nostrand Reinhold Ltd., 1981.

Crépeau, Pierre et al. *From the Heart: Folk Art in Canada.* Toronto: McClelland and Stewart with the National Museum of Man, National Museums of Canada, 1983.

Crépeau, Pierre. *Playing with the Wind.* Ottawa: The Canadian Museum of Civilization, 1991.

Crépeau, Pierre. *Pointing at the Wind.* Ottawa: the Canadian Museum of Civilization, 1990.

de Grosbois, Louise, Raymond Lamothe, and Lise Nantel. *Les patenteux du Québec.* Montréal: Parti pris, 1974.

Einarsson, Magnús, and Helga Benndorf Taylor, eds. *Just for Nice: German-Canadian Folk Art.* Ottawa: Canadian Museum of Civilization, 1993.

Folk Art of Nova Scotia: A Travelling Exhibition of the Folk Art of Nova Scotia. Halifax, N.S.: Art Gallery of Nova Scotia, 1977.

Galipeau, Pascale et al. *Les Paradis du monde. L'art populaire du Québec.* Ottawa: Canadian Museum of Civilization, 1995.

Grassroots Saskatchewan. Regina: Norman Mackenzie Art Gallery, 1976.

Harper, J. Russell. "Folk Sculpture of Rural Quebec: The Nettie Sharpe Collection." *Antiques* 103 (April 1973): 724–33.

Harper, J. Russell. *People's Art: Naïve Art in Canada.* Ottawa: National Gallery of Canada, 1973.

Inglis, Stephen. *Something out of Nothing: The Work of George Cockayne.* National Museum of Man, Mercury Series, Canadian Centre for Folk Culture Studies Paper #46. Ottawa: National Museums of Canada, 1983.

Klamkin, Charles. *Weather Vanes: The History, Manufacture and Design of an American Folk Art.* New York: Hawthorn Books, 1973.

Neal, Avon, and Ann Parker. *Ephemeral Folk Figures: Scarecrows, Harvest Figures and Snowmen.* New York: Clarkson N. Potter Inc., 1969.

Sloane, Eric. *Eric Sloane's America.* New York: Promontory Press, 1954.

Tilney, Philip V. R. *Artifacts from the CCFCS: Sampling #1.* National Museum of Man, Mercury Series, Canadian Centre for Folk Culture Studies Paper #5. Ottawa: National Museums of Canada, 1973.

GARDENING

Aird, Louise. "The 'A' Team of Canadian Landscape Architecture." *Landscape Trades* (June 1991): 12–21.

The American Lawn. Surface of Everyday Life. Exhibition brochure for exhibition of same name. Montreal: Canadian Centre for Architecture, 1998.

Cruso, Thalassa. *Making Things Grow. A Practical Guide for the Indoor Gardener.* New York: Alfred A. Knopf, 1969.

Douglas, W. L., S. R. Frey, N. K. Johnson, S. Litlefield, and M. Van Valkenburgh. *Garden Design: History, Principles, Elements, Practice.* New York: Simon and Schuster, 1984.

Hobhouse, Penelope, ed. *Gertrude Jekyll on Gardening: An Anthology.* London: Macmillan, 1983.

Jay, Roni. *Gardens of the Spirit. Create Your Own Sacred Spaces.* New York: Sterling Publishing Company Inc., 1998.

Jenkins, Virginia Scott. *The Lawn: The History of an American Obsession.* Washington, D.C.: Smithsonian Institution Press, 1994.

Milovsoroff, Ann. "For the Love of Gardens: A Biography of H.B. and L.A. Dunington-Grubb." *Canadian Horticultural History/Histoire de l'horticulture au Canada* 2, no. 3 (1990): 101–133.

Plumptre, George. *The Garden Makers: The Great Tradition of Garden Design from 1600 to the Present Day.* London: Pavilion Books Limited, 1993.

Schama, Simon. *Landscape and Memory.* New York: Alfred A. Knopf, 1995.

von Baeyer, Edwinna. *Rhetoric and Roses: A History of Canadian Gardening 1900–1930.* Markham, Ontario: Fitzhenry & Whiteside, 1984.

Wirth, Thomas. *The Victory Garden Landscape Guide.* Boston: Little Brown and Company, 1984.

Wydra, Nancilee. *Feng Shui in the Garden: Simple Solutions for Creating Comforting, Life-Affirming Gardens of the Soul.* Chicago: Contemporary Books, 1997.

HERBALS

Beston, Henry. *Herbs and the Earth.* Garden City, N.Y.: 1935.

Bishop, Carol. *The Book of Home Remedies and Herbal Cures.* London: Octopus Books Limited, 1979.

Boland, Bridget. *Gardener's Magic and Other Old Wives' Lore.* New York: Farrar Straus Giroux, 1977.

Bolton, Brett L. *The Secret Powers of Plants.* London: Abacus, 1975.

Duff, Gail. *Country Wisdom: An Encyclopedia of Recipes and Traditional Good Sense.* London: Pan Books Limited, 1979.

Griffith-Jones, Joy. *The Virtuous Weed.* London: Blond & Briggs, 1977.

Jarvis, D.C., M.D. *Folk Medicine.* Greenwich, Conn.: Fawcett Publications Inc., 1958.

McDowell, Ruth B. *Seventeenth Century New England Garden Herbs.* Saugus, Mass.: Saugus Iron Works National Historic Site, n.d.

Thomson, William A.R., and Elizabeth Smith. *Healing Herbs.* London: British Broadcasting Corporation, 1978.